Cadillac
Standard of Excellence

BY THE EDITORS OF CONSUMER GUIDE®

CASTLE BOOKS

Contents

Library of Congress Catalog Card Number: 80-81207

This edition published by:
Castle Books
A Division of Book Sales, Inc.
110 Enterprise Avenue
Secaucus, N.J. 07094

Chief Contributing Author: Richard M. Langworth
Contributing Authors: Jeffrey I. Godshall, Walter E. Gosden,
Gwilym G. Griffiths, Roy A. Schneider

Cover Design: Frank E. Peiler

Introduction

Of all the American *grand marques,* Cadillac has survived the longest. For 77 years now, the company has been turning out some of the finest cars in the world. Ironically, Cadillacs have probably been underrated simply because there are so many of them on the road.

Cadillac has done so much over the years in styling and engineering that we're inclined to forget its commercial importance in the automobile industry. Though never among the production leaders, Cadillac has built luxury cars in such high numbers that other manufacturers might blanch with envy. Its annual output is greater than the combined total for *all* other luxury cars sold in America, domestic and imported.

This book traces the steps along the way to this unequalled level of success: The single-cylinder cars of the early 1900s, which sounded the death-knell for the hand-built automobile; the four-cylinder Model Thirty, the success of which brought Cadillac into General Motors; the revolu-tionary V-8 of 1915 and its stylish successors of the late '20s and '30s; the magnificent V-16 and V-12 "supercars" of motoring's golden age; and the trend-setting 60 Special of 1938. Here, too, are all the spectacular post-World War II Cadillacs, which in their time turned the automotive world upside down: The beautiful 1948 tailfin model; the overhead-valve V-8 cars and the Coupe deVille hardtop of 1949; the first Eldorado of 1953; the air-suspension 1957 Eldorado Brougham; 1967's su-perlative front-wheel-drive Eldorado; the compact Seville of 1975; and the latest jewel in Cadillac's crown, the 1980 Seville.

This is a success story—the story of "An American Standard for the World." And regardless of the qualifications by which auto slogans are usually judged, Cadillac has been just that for four generations. If you doubt it, just turn the page and start reading. Even if you already agree, start reading anyway—there are more reasons for this claim than you ever imagined.

"Stamped With the Seal of Genius" 1903-1929

Henry Martyn Leland

Henry Martyn Leland was 60 years old when he formed Cadillac, and 74 when he founded the Lincoln Motor Company. That says much about this many-faceted man. Until his death in 1932, Leland was the very picture of fitness. Born in Vermont in 1843, he was a lifelong Republican wedded to old-fashioned virtues (he abstained from both tobacco and drink). Leland's humor was typical of a New Englander—subtle, but with a dry bite. He once told Jordan's founder, Ned Jordan, that a young man had basically two choices in his career: "If he chooses to be clever, he will meet with a great deal of competition. If he chooses to be just plain old-fashioned honest and industrious, he will be so unique he will make an almost immediate success."

Young Henry's early years were spent as an apprentice at the Federal Arsenal at Springfield, Massachusetts. There, and later at the Colt Arms Company and Brown & Sharpe, he learned the skills that would eventually earn him the title "Master of Precision." Almost from the start he was attracted to the concept of interchangeable parts in all things mechanical. Less than 10 years after he took over Cadillac, he would amaze the world by building an automobile that could be completely disassembled and then rebuilt using parts from another car.

In 1890, Leland set up his own machining factory in Detroit, and soon expanded into foundry work for the infant horseless carriage industry. One of his major assignments was building engines for Ransom E. Olds' whimsical curved-dash runabout, the world's first true production car and the country's single most popular model from 1903 through 1905. Also in those early years, the firm which eventually would become Cadillac was struggling to survive. It was established in 1899 as the Detroit Automobile Company.

D.A.C. had not been successful, and in 1901 had been reorganized as the Henry Ford Company, with none other than the wizard of Dearborn in charge. But Ford quit after just 3 weeks, and went on to greater things. His successors approached Leland and asked him to appraise the firm before deciding whether to continue with it. Leland persuaded them to hang on and recapitalize the ailing business—*and* to let his own company supply a precision-made one-cylinder engine he'd been working on. In 1904, after a disastrous fire (but in the face of rising demand for their cars), company owners made Leland general manager. The revitalized firm's first effort (produced beginning in September, 1902) was the Cadillac Model A, the first in a long line of cars which would become the envy of the industrialized world.

The firm now adopted a new name inspired by the founder of Detroit, Le Sieur Antoine de la Mothe Cadillac. Soon, it appropriated his coat of arms as its symbol. Two centuries earlier, this explorer had arrived at a place in New France which

1903 Model A—the first Cadillac

RICHARD M. LANGWORTH

he named Ville d'Etroit (Village of the Straights). So, Cadillac was an appropriate—perhaps even the *perfect*—name for a car and a new automobile company.

The Model A Cadillac (and the one-cylinder Models B, C, E, F, K, M, S, and T which followed through 1908) was in no sense a luxury car. Unlike the vaunted Pierce Great Arrow which sold for up to $5000, the first Cadillac was a modest-looking runabout priced at only $750. Whimsical ads promoted it with phrases like, "It's Just Good All Over," or "By Long Odds the Best Proposition Yet Offered." Designed along the lines of contemporary Fords and Oldsmobiles, it used a horizontal engine with a rear-mounted cylinder head and had a two-speed planetary gearbox.

The early Cadillacs were more expensive than Oldsmobiles of the period and were more advanced in some features. For instance, Cadillac used a steering wheel instead of a tiller, and mounted a spring at each wheel instead of using a leaf spring at each side of the chassis. The first Ford engine was a parallel twin, while Cadillac's was a single-cylinder unit; Ford used elliptical springs while Cadillac at first preferred semi-elliptics. But like the first Fords, the early Cadillacs were designed to meet the most pressing need of the day: a reasonably priced, reliable mechanical carriage that would get people out of their buggies and off their horses. The Model A easily did just that. Its engine displaced 98.2 cubic inches and developed about 10 horsepower. One-lung Cadillacs would do as much as 45 mph and return about 25 miles per gallon of gas. (Interestingly, Cadillac's mileage has since come full circle: 25 mpg is now a goal which its cars of the '80s can certainly reach, yet they will still be among the largest and most luxurious in the world.)

In the annals of the auto industry, there are several achievements which stand out as milestones of technical progress. Perhaps the greatest of these is the assembly-line method of production, begun in 1902 by Ransom Olds, and greatly expanded in 1908 when Henry Ford started turning out his Model T in unheard of numbers. Another milestone is the use of interchangeable parts, made possible by standardization of manufacturing methods so that all parts of a particular type would be exactly alike. In those distant years, the idea of pulling a part off a shelf and fitting it as a replacement to an existing engine was unheard of. Instead, bits and pieces were laboriously and individually hand-fitted. Everything in Leland's background argued against this—and so did his common sense. From the beginning, he had stressed the concept of parts interchangeability. "No special fitting of any kind is permitted," he wrote in a factory manual. "Craftsmanship a Creed, Accuracy a Law." In 1908, Leland became the first industrialist to employ Johannson

1904 single-cylinder engine

1907 Model K runabout

1908 Model S runabout

gauges for checking the accuracy of his tooling. These devices were extremely accurate blocks which measured tolerances down to two-millionths of an inch. Johannson gauges were not in widespread use when Cadillac won its first Dewar Trophy, so they symbolize Leland's concern with manufacturing precision. Frederick S. Bennett was the man who proved it.

Bennett was a British distributor for Cadillac—a fellow who regularly poked fun at the products of his native England and those of the European continent, neither of which he felt could hold a candle to Cadillac in production accuracy. In 1908, Bennett entered three randomly selected Cadillacs in a "Standardization Test" sponsored by the Royal Automobile Club. This involved first,

1907 Model G touring car

dismantling the cars completely, and then mixing up the parts from one with those of the others. Next, the parts were sorted back into three separate heaps, from which the three cars could then be reassembled. After the cars had been rebuilt, they were rolled out for a test run on the

Brooklands Motor Course, each a patchwork of different-colored doors, hoods, and other body panels, as well as various mechanical pieces. Dubious by-standers nicknamed these cars "the harlequins," but all three ran perfectly. Eight months later, the RAC awarded its Dewar Trophy to Cadillac for "the greatest achievement of the year." It was the first time a foreign car had won the honor. Leland had a fitting rejoinder: He adopted a new slogan, "Standard of the World." It soon became Cadillac's motto.

Even before those three single-cylinder cars won the Dewar Trophy, Henry Leland was busying himself with a Cadillac four. In the early 1900s, there was already a general trend in the industry toward multi-cylinder engines, and Cadillac would not be left behind. Its first such engine was a 300-cubic-inch unit for a car designated the Model D, of which 156 were built in 1905. This was followed by the similar Model H (1906-08), the 393-cid Model L (1906), and the 226-cid Model G (1907-08).

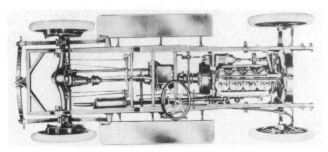

1913 ladder-type chassis

1911 "Thirty" 286.3-cid four-cylinder engine

1911 "Thirty" four-door touring car

1911 "Thirty" coupe

1913 Cadillac limousine

1912 Cadillac roadster

All these powerplants were of L-head configuration. Like the later single-cylinder engines, the early fours used a planetary transmission with three (instead of two) speeds, although the Model G switched to a selective sliding-gear three-speed transmission for its run of 629 cars.

None of the early Cadillac Fours were inexpensive (prices ranged from $2000 to $5000), so they sold sparingly. Also, a business recession in 1907 further reduced the market for really high-priced cars. Cadillac's response to this was typical of the Yankee ingenuity it had shown in its every move thus far. Its engineers simply took the best features of the firm's most efficient four-cylinder car, the Model G, and refined them for a much less expensive model, the Cadillac Thirty (named for its horsepower). As a result, sales improved to around 10,000 units annually, more than twice the best yearly output for the single-cylinder models which were now dropped. This sales increase put Cadillac in a strong financial position and resulted in a $2 million annual profit.

The Thirty's engine, based on that of the Model G, had a five-main-bearing crankshaft, induction coil and jump-spark ignition with optional magneto, float-feed carburetor, and automatic splash lubrication. It retained the selective sliding-gear three-speed transmission from the Model G. The Thirty's chassis was a simplified version of the G's designed with production economies in mind; for example, it employed flatter platform-type springs instead of elliptic-spring suspension. But the Thirty was six inches longer in wheelbase, at 106 inches, compared to the Model G's 100 inches.

Immediately, Cadillac advertising sprang to the attack. "1/1000ths of an inch is the standard of measurement in the Cadillac 'Thirty,'" the ads read. "What is the peculiar quality in any motor car for which you pay $5,000 or $6,000?" The pitch worked—largely because, with its initial price of $1400, the Thirty was one of the great automotive bargains of its day.

As the years passed, the Thirty grew gradually in price, size, and power. Closed bodies were soon added (Cadillac was a pioneer in this respect), but because of the very complex and detailed construction methods of the day, they were expensive: Prices reached up to $3250 for a seven-passenger limousine. In 1912, the "Thirty" designation was dropped and the cars were known simply as Cadillacs. This move reflected the model's increased horsepower, made possible by progressively larger engine displacements: 255.3 cid in 1910, 286.3 cid in 1911. The 286 engine delivered 40 brake horsepower.

Like the last of the single-cylinder cars, the last of the Cadillac Fours won great laurels for the marque: In 1913, the Royal Automobile Club presented Cadillac with its second Dewar Trophy. This time it was in honor of the Delco system of

1913 four-passenger torpedo

electric starting, lighting, and ignition, developed by Leland and Charles F. Kettering of the Dayton Engineering Laboratories. The Delco system was a breakthrough almost as important as interchangeable parts: It was the forerunner of the automobile electrical system as we know it today. A second noteworthy innovation came in 1914 with Cadillac's two-speed rear axle, which provided an effective six speeds forward. This gave the car great flexibility—strong pulling power at low speeds and relatively silent cruising at higher speeds. When geared to the axle's lower numerical ratio of 2.5:1, the engine of a Cadillac Thirty turned at just 1400 rpm at 60 mph.

It was 1908 when Cadillac first caught the attention of William Crapo Durant, the founder of General Motors. A brilliant amalgamator and speculator, Durant was the man who first envisioned the "diversified product line" form of marketing, an idea which would make GM the industry's dominant force in later years. Almost

William C. Durant—founder of General Motors

Henry Leland (at wheel) with son Wilfred (right)

alone among his contemporaries, Billy Durant could see the advantage of a corporation composed of several divisions, each building a car designed for a specific price sector of the market. Durant started building this sort of company in 1904 by buying Buick. That ever-successful auto maker produced sufficiently good returns that he was able to acquire the Olds Motor Works in 1908. That same year, Durant's desire for a high-quality product aimed at the price range just above Buick led him to offer Leland $3 million for Cadillac.

Leland's son Wilfred, a fine engineer in his own right, acted as Cadillac's negotiator in the discussions with Durant. Wilfred held out for $3.5 million. Durant declined, but after the Thirty arrived and began selling well, he was back at Leland's doorstep. This time, the canny Vermonter replied that the asking price was now $4.125 million. Durant hesitated, and Wilfred upped the ante again to $4.5 million! Durant realized he was playing a no-win game. He accepted that figure and actually paid in *cash*, using money he'd earned from Buick. He also invited the Lelands to continue running Cadillac "exactly as though it were your own." This they did until 1917, when they left to form the Lincoln Motor Company which, like Cadillac, built Liberty aircraft engines for the U.S. government.

Though partly eclipsed in the history books by his father, Wilfred Leland played a strong managerial and engineering role at Cadillac after its acquisition by General Motors. For example, in 1910 Durant became over-extended, and his bankers considered dissolving GM simply to save Buick; Wilfred singlehandedly convinced them that Cadillac deserved to be rescued, too. In 1916, Durant regained control of GM, but he had become less a manager than a visionary, and eventually was eased out of company affairs by the duPont interests in 1920. By then, Cadillac had

become so well established financially that its survival was never questioned. According to Alfred P. Sloan, who became GM president in 1923, Buick and Cadillac were the firm's only profitable divisions at that time. They remained GM's number one and two sellers while, under Sloan's management, a vast reorganization took place in the lower-price lines.

Although Wilfred Leland had suggested the idea of a Cadillac V-8 engine as early as 1912, the man most responsible for this breakthrough was engineer D. McCall White. White was a Scotsman who had trained at Daimler and Napier in Britain, and his experience there undoubtedly influenced him. Development of Cadillac's V-8 began in great secrecy during the summer of 1913: The engine was introduced with tremendous publicity just 15 months later.

Of course, the V-8 configuration was not a new idea even in those days, but it had never been commercially viable: Cadillac was the first to make it so. Latterday skeptics have occasionally suggested that the Cadillac engine was a mere copy of the De Dion V-8 (the most significant of the Cadillac's predecessors). But that powerplant merely gave Cadillac engineers a basis from which to develop their own design. Its principal advantages over the De Dion engine included far more effective cooling, stronger-yet-lighter main components, and easier serviceability.

1914 Cadillac roadster

The first V-8 production engine, 1915

The V-8 layout was adopted for reasons which have remained in vogue for half a century. It provided smoothness equal to that of the big straight sixes then favored by luxury-car makers, but its greater compactness would permit more of the car's overall length to be used for passenger space. Cadillac's first V-8 model had a 122-inch wheelbase, although its passenger room rivaled cars with wheelbases up to a foot longer. The engine's lighter reciprocating parts and its lighter-but-stiffer crankshaft were additional benefits of the design. The cylinders were arranged in a 90-degree V; bore and stroke were 3.13 x 5.13 inches for 314 cubic inches and 70 bhp at 2400 rpm. This translated to a top speed of 55-60 mph. Naturally, the car also featured the Delco electrical system, now updated with a generator and storage battery. Cadillac abandoned the selective sliding-gear transmission in favor of a multiple-disc/dry-plate clutch, though the gearbox was still a three-speed unit with final drive ratios of 4.45 and 5.08. The frame was an H-type with side rails and a transverse center bar, reinforced by tubular cross members. Steering was by worm-and-sector and mechanical brakes worked on the rear wheels. Initially, ten body styles were available including closed models, with prices from $2000 to $3600.

Cadillac produced 13,000 of its 1915 Type 51 V-8, volume which was on a par with the company's four-cylinder days. But from 1916 through the end of this first-generation V-8 in 1923, model year production was usually around 20,000 units. In 1922, it hit 26,296, and only in the recession year of 1921 did output drop seriously.

The Cadillacs which descended from the Type 51 (Models 53, 55, 57, 59, and 61, produced through 1923) were all similar in body design. They were relatively short cars, with some hint of streamlining. All had flat dashboards and small, short doors. Evolutionary engineering changes continued to enhance the product. Horsepower gradually rose, reaching 79 bhp by 1920. Wheelbases grew longer to meet customer demand: 125 and 132 inches in 1917, 132 inches across-the-board in 1921. Selling in the price bracket between $2000 and $5000, these were the cars that made Cadillac a force in the fine-car field. Writing in *Car Classics* magazine in 1977, Cadillac historian Maurice D. Hendry noted: "The V-8 sounded the death-knell of the highly specialized, high-priced, hand-made car . . . V-8 production/sales figures hovered around ten times those of, say, Pierce-Arrow or Locomobile." Hendry quoted W. A. Robotham of Rolls-Royce, who wrote that the American Rolls-Royce operation failed because it was "faced with very severe competition from the V-8 Cadillac and the V-12 Packard—quality cars fitted with every conceivable accessory, followed by the V-8 Lincoln and Peerless—all good cars selling at an

1915 Type 51 sedan

1915 Type 51 coupe

1916 Type 53 five-passenger convertible

1916 Type 53 seven-passenger touring car

1917 Type 55 victoria

1917 Type 55 coupe

1918-19 Type 57 seven-passenger limousine

1917 Type 55 seven-passenger landaulet

1918-19 Type 57 town landaulet

1918 Type 57 five-passenger brougham

U.S. Army Type 57 seven-passenger touring car

astonishingly low price because of the large quantity involved."

Though the Lelands left in 1917, Cadillac benefitted from the influence of other imaginative engineers, such as Benjamin H. Anibal from 1917 to 1923, and Ernest W. Seaholm from early 1923 to 1943. Seaholm was on hand during what many consider the greatest period in Cadillac's technical development. His 20 years with the division saw the arrival of the inherently balanced V-8, the V-16 and V-12 engines, and the beginnings of the modern overhead-valve V-8, which would appear in 1949.

The inherently balanced V-8 was another contribution of that great technician, Charles F. Kettering. Its two-plane crankshaft eliminated a peculiar roughness period common in all early V-8s. Even Cadillac's first V-8s with their superbly balanced one-plane cranks had been plagued by this vibration at certain engine speeds. The inherently balanced V-8 was introduced for the 1924 V-63 model. Another standard had been set for the division, and for the world's automotive industry.

The V-63's other revolutionary feature was Cadillac's first use of four-wheel brakes, which most other manufacturers wouldn't adopt until several years later. Internal expanding bands were used on the front wheels, and separate hand or foot brakes operated on the rear wheels. The front and rear brakes were pressure-equalized.

Cadillac hardly had time to catch its breath in its headlong rush of innovation. For 1926-27, it offered the Series 314 (named for its engine displacement), with a new, lighter, stronger, and more powerful V-8 developed by Owen Nacker. This engine developed 86 bhp at 3000 rpm, and made the 314 the quickest Cadillac yet. Published figures by division engineers show the sedan model could achieve close to 70 mph, and accelerate from 10 to 25 mph in high gear in 7.1 seconds. The lighter open models would do commensurately better.

The Series 314 marked the beginning of another trend which was somewhat overshadowed by the car's stunning mechanical features. The 1927 version (the 314-A) was the first Cadillac to show

10

signs of what we now call "styling." This was due to the presence of Harley Earl, a gifted California custom body designer who had been brought to Detroit by Fred Fisher of the famous Fisher brothers, long-time builders of Cadillac bodies. Earl's main attention for 1927 was directed to Cadillac's newly announced companion car, LaSalle (see Chapter III), but he did not overlook the Cadillac entirely. For too long, GM's prestige marque with its staid, upright lines had lagged behind Packard in design. This, perhaps, was a legacy left by Cadillac's founders. Indeed, when the Lelands began building Lincolns in 1920, they used the same kind of honest-but-homely bodies as Cadillac had. This problem lingered on at Lincoln even after it was acquired by Henry Ford.

Harley Earl didn't have time to fully redesign the 1927 Cadillac. But he did conjure up 50 different custom and factory body styles and no less than 5000 color combinations. A smart new walnut veneer dash with German silver inlay appeared. The following year's Series 341 featured LaSalle-like lines end to end. Thus was born the first Cadillac of the golden age: long, svelte, sleek—a car of elegant proportions with nary a line out of place. The upright look of the late "Teens" had been replaced with classic styling which, for the first time, fearlessly challenged the luxury leader, Packard.

By any measure, 1928 was a banner year. The magnificent 341 led Cadillac to record sales volume. Model year production was an even 40,000 units—56,000 counting LaSalle output. For the calendar year, which included some 1929 models, combined production was 41,172 units. Sales were down only slightly in 1929, and it looked like a new era of progress and profits had dawned. Then came October—and Black Tuesday.

In light of the serious losses suffered by the world economy after the Great Crash, it may come as a surprise to note that General Motors never lost money throughout the Depression. This was due to managerial efficiency, plus the philosophy of strict product diversification and market concentration preached by GM president Alfred P. Sloan. Cadillac, however, was in a precarious position. Dedicated as it was to the market sector at the upper end of the price scale, the division faced a potentially drastic decrease in sales. Indeed, production sank to a mere 6000 units in 1933, including LaSalle.

That Cadillac emerged from the Depression at all is a tribute to its leaders, beginning with its general manager from 1925-34, Lawrence P. Fisher. The make's survival is even more extraordinary in view of the tremendous investment which had been poured in a new super-automobile for 1930. Given the economic conditions of the Depression, the mighty V-16 was precisely the wrong product at the wrong time. Today, its status as an automobile is among the highest.

1920 Type 59 roadster

1920-21 Type 59 "Suburban"

1920 Type 59 seven-passenger touring car

1923 Type V-63 touring car

"A Masterpiece Will Set a Million Tongues A-Wagging" V-16 and V-12

A sampling of 1931 V-16 body styles

Choosing a fashionable automobile was a fairly serious matter for wealthy Americans in the '20s. In those days, most luxury cars were powered by massive sixes and eights which got increasingly larger displacements as the decade wore on. This was needed to ensure adequate power with the low compression ratios in use at the time. Unfortunately, the larger cylinder displacements magnified inherent engine vibration stemming from various internal combustion forces. As a result, reducing noise, vibration, and passenger fatigue became a real engineering problem. Hence, the great American race toward inherently smoother multi-cylinder engines, which culminated in the supercars of the early '30s.

In the view of many historians, the Cadillac V-16 was the most significant powerplant to emerge during these years. It preceded every other domestic multi-cylinder engine by at least a year—and it was a *sixteen*, not a twelve or a glorified eight. With it, Cadillac capitalized on tremendous international interest in multi-cylinder supercars. In fact, Cadillac was the only company that really profited with such a car. Before buyer demand tailed off in mid-1930, the division had shipped over 2000 V-16s, more than the entire three-year production run of the fabulous Marmon Sixteen.

Owen Milton Nacker was largely responsible for engineering the Cadillac V-16 engine. Lawrence P. Fisher had recruited Nacker from outside the GM organization expressly to design this powerplant. He brought considerable experience and aptitude to Cadillac's engine design section. With Fisher, Nacker contrived to make the rest of the industry think Cadillac was working on a V-12 instead. From statements by former executives of competing firms, this ruse was a complete success. Nacker actually designed the V-12 and the V-16 together, which accounts for the wide parts interchangeability between the two. But all the technical drawings and requests for price quotes, at least those seen outside Nacker's office, referred only to a 12-cylinder configuration. However, it was the V-16 that was introduced first—and with suitable fanfare—in January, 1930. The V-12 that appeared the following September took a back seat in publicity.

1930-38 ohv V-16—452 cid, 175 bhp

Massive and beautiful, the mechanism under the hoods of those first Series 452 and 452A V-16 cars was a visually satisfying study in enamel, chrome, porcelain, and polished aluminum. A giant cast-aluminum crankcase cradled separate, straight eight-cylinder blocks splayed at 45 degrees. Cylinder heads were capped with intricately detailed valve covers. The engine had unobtrusive outboard manifolding, concealed wiring, and discreetly placed accessories. All this "engine styling" was certainly unique, and reflected Cadillac's concern with making the powerplant's appearance as pleasing as possible. (Similar styling was carried out on the companion L-head V-8 of 1930-31, which had dust covers over its cylinder heads to hide wiring. The shape of these covers suggested an overhead-valve layout.)

Sixteen small cylinders, each with a three-inch bore and a four-inch stroke, yielded 452 cubic inches of displacement. Quoted power output was 175 bhp at 3400 rpm, though dynamometer tests conducted at the factory actually indicated close to 200 bhp when measured with contemporary test stand techniques. The compensated crankshaft was supported in five large bearings and was no longer than that of any contemporary eight-cylinder powerplant. Inertia forces were minimal and bearing loads were limited to the weight of the parts and the power impulses. The forged carbon-steel crankshaft weighed 130 pounds and was painstakingly balanced to eliminate torsional vibration; residual vibration was absorbed by a harmonic balancer.

The silicon-aluminum alloy crankcase was heat treated for maximum strength and suspended in the frame at five points. Each mount was cushioned in rubber. The V-16's connecting rods were drop-forged from molybdenum steel and designed for sustained performance at high speeds. Lubrication to the lower con-rod bearings was provided through metered holes in the crankshaft. Nickel-iron pistons were featured in the first several editions; using the same material for both pistons and cylinder blocks assured equal expansion and avoided electrolysis problems. Closely fitted, the pistons were designed for quiet operation without scuffing; on the 1930 Series 452 they employed three compression rings at the top and one oil ring at the bottom.

Detachable heads incorporated valves and rocker arms operated from the camshaft by pushrods. A 5.5:1 compression ratio was standard in early 1930, but lower-ratio head gaskets were available. The ohv design made servicing a Cadillac V-16 considerably easier than on the competitive L-head twelves which appeared in 1932.

A single distributor with two sets of contact points was designed especially for the V-16. Current was provided by dual coils, initially mounted atop the radiator tank where they were protected

1930 Series 452 Fleetwood V-16 Landaulette

1931 Series 452A Fleetwood V-16 five-passenger phaeton

RICHARD M. LANGWORTH

from engine heat. Spark advance was controlled by an automatic governor regulated by engine speed, a Cadillac feature since 1906. Since it was seldom required, the spark control was relocated from its customary place on the steering wheel to the instrument board.

Cadillac took pains with the V-16's cooling system, which had a seven-gallon capacity, large water passages, and a big centrifugal pump. Lubrication was also carefully planned. The V-16 had a 10-quart sump with a floating sight gauge on the crankcase. The unique and dependable fuel system used one vacuum tank and a carburetor for each cylinder bank. The tanks operated from manifold vacuum, assisted by a mechanical vacuum pump to provide fuel feed under all conditions. The carburetors were a variation on the Cadillac-built units in use for some years before the V-16 arrived, though an automatic fuel pump and Detroit lubricator carb appeared in 1932.

The inevitable questions about the V-16 are how fast it would propel the car and how many miles it would deliver per gallon of gas. Speed, of course, was determined by body style, vehicle weight, and rear axle ratio. The lowest numerical ratio offered with the V-16 in 1930 was 3.47:1 (dropped in mid-year because high-speed driving was impractical on most roads of the day) and the lightest body was the roadster. This combination would yield over 100 mph. More typical, however, would be a car with a seven-passenger body weighing close to 6500 pounds. Equipped with a 4.07:1 rear axle

1931 Series 370A Fleetwood V-12 all-weather phaeton

1931 Series 370A V-12 two-passenger coupe

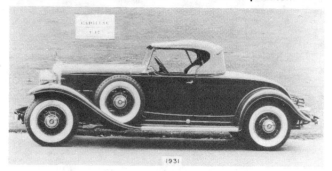

1931 Series 370A V-12 roadster

1932 Series 370B V-12 town car

ratio, this model would have a top speed of just over 90 mph. Mileage figures were about the same as those for some full-size station wagons of the late '60s: 8 mpg around town, 10 mpg on the road. But then, the V-16 owner was probably the sort who did not need to be too concerned about economy.

Considered in the context of contemporary engineering art and the burgeoning luxury-car market of 1929, the V-16 represented the ultimate powerplant of the Classic age. But that was only part of the story: Coachwork also played a major

role in the success of Cadillac's supercar. The exotic styling and lavish appointments that dominated Fleetwood offerings for 1930 and subsequent years were hard to match among rival luxury makes. Of course, there was a family resemblance among all Cadillacs of the '30s. The V-16s looked like corresponding V-12 and V-8 models except that they were longer and more luxurious.

Initially, there were 20 Fleetwood bodies offered for the V-16 Series 452/452A. These included a roadster, phaetons, cabriolets, coupes, sedans,

1932 Series 452B V-16 seven-passenger sedan

14

1933 Series 370C Fleetwood V-12 seven-passenger sedan

1934 Series 452D Fleetwood V-16 two-passenger coupe

1935 Series 370D V-12 five-passenger touring sedan

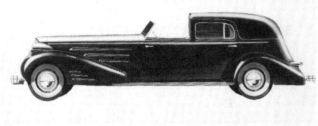

1935 Series 452D Fleetwood V-16 town car

Imperial sedans, and limousines priced from around $5500 to $7500. The most interesting of these were those with "Madam X" coachwork with rakishly sloped one-piece or vee'd windshields. The name was suggested by Harley Earl after the mysterious lady character in a popular 1929 play. Some Madam X Cadillacs were distinguished by stainless steel striping instead of the usual painted striping; some even had gold-faced instruments and stainless steel spoked wire wheels. The largest number of Madam X models was offered in 1930-31 when 12 styles in sedan, cabriolet, Imperial, town car, and coupe form were on the books. An Imperial cabriolet and Imperial sedan (models 5555 and 5556) were the Madam X listings for 1933. There was also one V-12 car (the five-passenger Imperial cabriolet, model 5455) in this configuration.

As mentioned, the Cadillac V-12 was introduced six months after the V-16. It was completely derived from the larger engine, except that it had a 3.13-inch, instead of a 3-inch, bore for a displacement of 368 cubic inches. With 135 bhp this smooth, relatively high-revving engine was not as powerful as its bigger brother, but it did give Cadillac a direct competitor for a gaggle of twelve-cylinder models from Packard, Lincoln, and lesser makes which followed in the early '30s. The V-12 series initially comprised 11 bodies priced from about $3800 to $4900 and always outsold the V-16.

After 1933, V-16 sales were miniscule: 56, 50, 52,

and 49 units for the 1934-37 model years, respectively. In 1938, the ohv design was replaced by an L-head version which took much of its technical inspiration from the L-head V-8s. Chief engineer Ernest W. Seaholm wrote a booklet on the new V-16, which described the reasons for abandoning the earlier ohv layout: "Since the total sales volume in this field is necessarily limited, a simplification was indicated. Also, development of the Cadillac V-8 engine [see Chapter IV] had progressed to the point where its power development was almost equal to that of the Twelve, and in power-to-weight ratio and general efficiency, the Eight was superior to both the Twelve and Sixteen.

"To realize the twofold purpose of simplification and improved engine design, the production of an entirely new model to supersede both the Twelve- and Sixteen-cylinder lines was decided upon; this model was to have a modern engine based upon the principles which had proven successful in the V-8." The design goals set for the L-head Sixteen were: (1) power output at least equal to that of the ohv V-16; (2) shorter length compared with the ohv V-12 and V-16; (3) lighter weight than either previous engine; (4) lower production costs than with the old V-16, along with easier maintenance; and (5) high standards of performance and serviceability.

The most visible difference in the new V-16 was its wide 135-degree angle between cylinder banks against the old engine's 45 degrees. These are the

1935 Series 452D V-16 convertible sedan

only two angles which give equal firing intervals and inherent running smoothness in a V-engine. The original V-16 had a valve-in-head design because its narrow "V" did not provide space for side valves, according to Seaholm: "Since simplification was one of our aims, we favored L-head combustion chambers and side valves operated by one camshaft in the center of the vee. The wider, 135 vee angle was, therefore, desirable for space requirements of the side valves ... the wider vee angle also was desirable in providing more length between cam and valve head. [It] provided more space for the manifolds and downdraft carburetors. The wide angle reduced engine height but increased width. There was, however, no objection to the width increase." (This was because Cadillac body designs were becoming wider, allowing more space under the hood.)

Seaholm determined that body and chassis design for the new model meant the L-head V-16's displacement would have to be around 430 cubic inches. Four configurations were then laid out for comparison of such factors as bore and stroke, crankshaft type, and bearing size:

Engine Number	1	2	3	4
bore	3.00″	3.13″	3.25″	3.25″
stroke	3.75″	3.50″	3.25″	3.25″
displacement	424 ci	429 ci	431 ci	431 ci
main bearings	five	five	five	nine
con-rod length	7.00″	6.50″	6.50″	6.38″

"Preliminary layouts indicated that engine No. 1 was the shortest but that engine No. 4 was almost as short and would be narrower and probably lighter," wrote Seaholm. "Engine No. 4 because of its short stroke and short, light connecting rod had the lowest connecting-rod bearing pressure-velocity factors. Its large bore caused a higher rod bearing load due to gas pressure, but this was thought of small importance since high gas pressures occur only at low speed. Tests were made which proved the higher

gas pressures did not reduce bearing life. In regard to crankshaft stresses, engine No. 4 also compared well.

"Other factors influenced us in choosing engine No. 4. Its short stroke reduced the height, width and weight of the engine. [And it was desirable] from the standpoint of low piston speed, which improves durability and oil economy." (With the standard axle ratio of 4.31:1, engine No. 3 had the shortest piston travel.)

The new compact V-16 achieved all the goals Seaholm had set out to meet. Its higher horsepower gave genuine 100-mph capability for more body types, yet its gas mileage was at least as good as that of the earlier engine. Cadillac's own figures showed 10-25 mph acceleration in 4.8 seconds and 10-60 mph in 16 seconds, times which were said to be better than those for any other American car of 1938-40.

Prices of the 1938 Series 90 V-16 started at around $5200 and worked their way up to about $7500. The usual broad range of Fleetwood bodies was offered, including sedans, Imperial sedans, convertible sedans, formal and town sedans, town car, coupes, convertible coupe, and a special 161-inch wheelbase "Presidential" model. But production was very low, even during years when the nation was slowly climbing out of its economic doldrums. Only 311 Series 90s were built for the 1938 model year. In 1939, production dropped to 136, and in 1940 it was only 61 units.

The rarest Series 90 body styles were the 1938 five-passenger Imperial sedan (5), five-passenger formal sedan (8), and five-passenger coupe (8); the 1939 five-passenger Imperial (2), town sedan (2), and formal sedan (4); the 1940 five-passenger town sedan (1), five-passenger coupe (1), town car, two-passenger coupe, five-passenger formal sedan, and convertible coupe (2 each). Obviously, most Sixteens were Imperial sedans, seven-passenger sedans, and limousines. This was not the kind of car purchased by the owner-driver, even if he or she was particularly well-heeled.

1936 Series 90 V-16 seven-passenger sedan

It was miniscule production which, in the end, condemned the V-16 to history. General manager Nicholas Dreystadt, who pushed hard for careful cost analysis and never let enthusiasm get in the way of common sense, was responsible for the decision. The Sixteen had been a loss-leader in all but its earliest years. Yet, what it proved was more important than profits.

The V-16 made it abundantly clear that Cadillac had "arrived" in the luxury field. To those who bought such exclusive carriages, it was the first time Cadillac had fielded a car so clearly superior to Packard. Indeed, Cadillac was the only company to make a sixteen-cylinder model that was even half-way profitable. To this extent, the V-16 was significant far beyond its low production numbers. Without doubt, it was an engineering masterpiece. And, as Theodore MacManus had predicted in "The Penalty of Leadership," it had clearly "set a million tongues a-wagging."

1937 Series 85 Fleetwood V-12 town car

1937 Series 85 V-12 town car

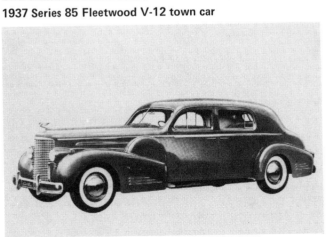

1940 Series 90 V-16 five-passenger town sedan

1940 Series 90 V-16 formal sedan

Many Cadillac connoisseurs consider the 1933 models to be the finest examples of what has come to be called motoring's "golden age." The '33 was a transition style—a blend of the old and the new. Yet it combines the best elements of each school.

This beautiful victoria represents the essence of the production Cadillac that year. In many ways, it is a throwback to earlier design ideas. Its trunk is a separate fixture, attached at the rear outside the main body structure; and it retains side-mount spare tires, though the more advanced Cadillac designs called for hidden spares. On the other hand, it displays skirted fenders with "speed lines," a prominent vee'd grille, and a fairly rakish windshield angle for the

time. Note in particular the beautiful and elegant four-bar bumpers carried by this car. They were found only on the 1933 models, and were probably inspired by the Chicago World's Fair fastback show car displayed that year. Unfortunately, these bumpers didn't stand up well in everyday use, so Cadillac replaced them with clumsy nerf-bar-and-bullet units in 1934, then reverted to conventionally sprung bumpers for 1935.

This is one of only 125 V-16s sold in 1933, a rock-bottom year when Cadillac produced only 6655 cars, including 3482 LaSalles. It's nice to know some of the better '33s have survived.

Car owned by W. F. Jahart. Photographs by Neil Perry.

"Long, Long After a Great Work Has Been Done" LaSalle, 1927-1940

Harley Earl, founder of GM styling

The latter part of the 1920s might be characterized as the era of the "companion car" at General Motors. In keeping with company policy of "a car in every price range," there were new supplemental offerings from every division except Chevrolet.

From Oakland came the Pontiac in 1926; from Olds, the Viking in 1929; from Buick, the Marquette in 1929; and from Cadillac, the LaSalle in 1927. Of all the newcomers, only Pontiac achieved lasting success. In fact, it became more popular than its Oakland sister, which was dropped after 1931. But of all the companion makes, the most romantic was LaSalle, the "junior Cadillac," which continued through 1940.

These new nameplates came about as the result of intensive studies undertaken in April, 1921 by a special committee composed of GM advisory staff and chaired by then executive vice-president Alfred P. Sloan. The group determined a car was clearly needed to fill the $1000 price gap between Buick and Cadillac, and decided that, of the two, Cadillac Division was better equipped to produce it. Choice of a suitable name was no problem. The name Cadillac had been chosen in honor of Antoine de la Mothe Cadillac, who founded Detroit in 1701. The name of another French explorer might be logical for the division's new model. The chosen pathfinder was Rene Robert Cavalier, Sieur de la Salle, who claimed the vast Louisiana territory for the King of France in 1682.

Introduced in March, 1927, the LaSalle was listed throughout its life as a Cadillac series. It was intended for the buyer looking for high quality and value in a smaller, less expensive, more maneuverable package. The company carefully stressed the car's Cadillac heritage. The

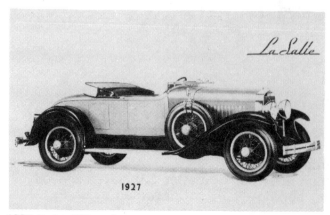

1927 Series 303 roadster

1927 Series 303 five-passenger sedan

20

catalogue proudly proclaimed the new LaSalle was of "genuine Cadillac calibre" and mechanically a "blood brother to the Cadillac." It was further stated that the new model was in no way an experiment. Rather, it came to the market only after four years of thorough research and testing.

The 1927 LaSalle Series 303 was offered with 22 body types. Eight of these—roadster, coupe, convertible coupe, four-passenger phaeton, dual-cowl sport phaeton, victoria, five-passenger sedan, and town sedan—stood on a 125-inch wheelbase, seven inches less than the shortest Cadillac chassis. For the more discriminating buyer, a series of Fleetwood bodies was available, including a two-passenger coupe, five-passenger sedan, town cabriolet, and transformable town cabriolet. Three special styles—the seven-passenger sedan, Imperial sedan, and five-passenger Imperial sedan—stood on a 134-inch wheelbase and carried Fisher coachwork.

Priced from $2495 to $2685 for the standard models, LaSalle fitted neatly between the most expensive Buick at $1995 and the cheapest Cadillac at $2995. Other cars in LaSalle's price range included the Chrysler Imperial 80, the Elcar 8-90, the Franklin Series 11-B, the Hupmobile Model E, the Jordan Great Line Eight, the Kissel 8-75, the little Marmon, the Packard Six, the Paige 8-85, the Peerless 6-72, and the Roamer 8-88. Though some of these were very low-volume products, all were quality automobiles. Perhaps LaSalle's greatest competition came from the Chrysler Imperial and the Packard Six, though the latter was dropped after 1928 when Packard lowered the price of its standard Eight. In any case, the newcomer faced a formidable array of established competitors, especially considering that its market sector was not much larger than Cadillac's.

The first LaSalle will be forever famous for its styling. It was not only a beautiful car in its own right, but also had an enormous impact on Cadillac styling from 1928 on. Its designer, of course, was Harley J. Earl, the Californian who had signed a consultant's contract with Cadillac early in 1926. It was a contract drawn up specifically with LaSalle in mind.

Harley Earl had grown up in his father's carriage shop, but he made his own reputation on the west coast as chief designer for the Don Lee studio. Cadillac general manager Lawrence P. Fisher was impressed with young Earl's total approach to car design. Earl used modeling clay to evolve the form of various body components, and in those days, clay was considered a highly unusual material for this purpose. Also, he created *complete* automobiles—the main body, hood, fenders, lights, and other parts were designed in relation to each other, blending into a unified whole. This was in contrast to most other custom body makers who usually worked from the cowl back while leaving a car's "stock" hood, radiator, and headlamps pretty much intact.

LaSalle, of course, was not primarily a custom-bodied product. But it was the first mass-produced car to be deliberately "styled," in the way we use the term today. That alone is enough to assure it a place in history.

The lines of the first LaSalle were somewhat reminiscent of the Hispano-Suiza—no surprise really, since Earl was quite familiar with European design trends of the day. In contrast to its square-cornered contemporaries, the LaSalle had graceful "tablespoon" fenders and smooth hood contours. On sedans, side windows were proportioned to provide a fleet look. Corners were rounded wherever possible. On some models, the hood and cowl were painted a darker shade than the main body. The result was an extremely successful, gracefully handsome car—a fact not lost on GM's astute management. Soon after he completed the LaSalle, Earl was invited by Alfred Sloan to work for GM full time with the specific task of establishing an in-house styling department. This was duly organized as the "Art and Colour Section" (Earl used the English spelling as a prestige note). Art and Colour was an industry first, and after 1927 the professional hand of the

1927-33 LaSalle L-head V-8

1927 Series 303 two-passenger coupe

stylist was increasingly evident in American auto design.

Mechanically, the 1927 LaSalle was a lighter, smaller Cadillac. Its 90-degree L-head V-8 had a bore and stroke of 3.13 x 4.94 inches for a displacement of 303 cubic inches (hence the series designation) and 75 bhp. Cadillac had built nearly 250,000 V-8s since its first one in 1915, and the LaSalle engine embodied that experience. It had three main bearings, detachable heads, and water-pump cooling via thermostatic radiator shutters. The car also had four-wheel mechanical brakes and a three-speed transmission as standard features.

LaSalle's durability and engineering excellence were demonstrated in a remarkable way at the then three-year old GM Proving Grounds in June, 1927. A standard roadster, taken right off the assembly line, was run 951 miles in 10 hours for an average speed of 95.1 mph. This car was completely stock except that its fenders, lamps, and running boards had been removed; its camshaft altered; and high-compression heads installed.

Driver 'Big Bill' Rader, who was in charge of GM's experimental garage, and riding mechanic Gus Bell made nine pit stops in all, halting the run after 10 hours only because of a ruptured oil line. This feat is even more remarkable when compared to the 1927 Indy 500, in which a 160-bhp Duesenberg won with an average speed a scant two mph faster—and covered only half as many miles. More impressive is the fact that 12 other production LaSalles were run over 300,000 miles without a single major failure during a four-month period in tests conducted by GM's experimental department. It was a performance that surpassed everyone's expectations. LaSalle was heartily accepted in the showrooms: Production of the Series 303 totalled an encouraging 26,807 units and Cadillac management was exceedingly pleased.

There was little need to change such a promising newcomer, so the 303 was continued without major alterations for 1928. Styling refinements included 28 small vertical hood louvers in place of the 12 louvers of 1927. Prices came down $155 on standard models, which now included five- and seven-passenger family sedans plus a four-passenger coupe. The Fleetwood line was expanded to include a four-passenger victoria, two passenger business coupe, five- and seven-passenger Imperials, five-passenger sedan, and fixed transformable.

More substantial changes were in order for 1929. The Series 328 (named for its bored out 328-cid V-8) adopted Cadillac's "silent synchromesh" transmission, plus new and improved internal four-wheel mechanical brakes, safety glass, and an adjustable front seat. Chromium plate replaced nickel plate on bright metal parts. Closed bodies stood on the 134-inch wheelbase,

1930 Series 340 sedanette cabriolet by Fleetwood

1930 Series 340 five-passenger sedan

1930 Series 340 Fleetway all-weather phaeton

while the 125-inch wheelbase chassis was reserved for open cars. Engines were dressed up with bright nickel fittings, nickeled acorn-head nuts, and a smooth black porcelain finish on the manifolds—a treatment that marked all LaSalles from first to last. Power output was 86 bhp.

Standard LaSalle bodies for '29 included four open and seven closed styles while the Fleetwood offerings boasted two different transformable cabriolets. Parking lights were moved to the top of the fenders. Prices ranged from $2345 for the two-passenger roadster to $2875 for the four-passenger sport phaeton, with Fleetwood bodies tagged at up to $4800. Production, however, dipped to 23,000 units, down 4000 from 1927. In the same price range, some 43,000 Packard Standard Eights were produced that year. LaSalle was not living up to its initial promise.

While Cadillac's big news in 1930 was the 452-cid V-16, LaSalle included among its improvements a 340-cid V-8 developing 90 bhp. Bore went to 3.31 inches, stroke remained the same,

1931 Series 345A five-passenger town sedan

1931 Series 345A two-passenger coupe

1931 Series 345A two-passenger convertible coupe

and high-compression (5.05:1) heads were standard. All bodies were new and all were now mounted on the 134-inch-wheelbase chassis. The seven standard Fisher styles were priced from $2375 to $2795, the six Fleetwood bodies from $2285 to $3795. Low-pressure, 20-inch balloon tires became standard, and steering was improved by changing front-axle geometry and adding a spring-loaded kick shackle at the front of one spring to minimize feedback. But again production fell—to 14,995 cars—a reflection of the country's failing economy.

In 1931, Cadillac had its new V-12, so LaSalle received only slight attention. That year's Series 345A offered 12 body styles on the 134-inch wheelbase and the cars now had 18-inch wheels and single-bar bumpers. By this time, LaSalle and the smallest Cadillac had become almost identical. They shared the same engine and chassis in line with management's desire for greater parts interchangeability among all GM lines to help keep production costs down. Though LaSalle

prices were cut by an average of $180, 1931 model year production slid to 10,103 cars.

New bodies graced the 1932 models, which had more rounded styling and graceful "flying wing" fenders. The Series 345B comprised four bodies on a 130-inch wheelbase and three on a 136-inch chassis. Engineering changes included decreased upsprung weight, synchromesh transmis-

1931 Series 345A two-passenger convertible coupe

sion, and adjustable two-way hydraulic shocks. Most interesting was an automatic, vacuum-operated clutch combined with freewheeling. The driver could disengage the clutch by pressing a button below the clutch pedal while letting up on the accelerator; it could then be engaged by releasing the button or by stepping on the gas. Of course, the clutch could also be used in the normal manner. LaSalle's 353 V-8 now developed 115 bhp. Prices ranged from $2394 to $2795, but production sagged again, to 3390 units. GM management now began to consider dropping the junior Cadillac, as the Marquette, Viking, and Oakland had been before it.

Nevertheless, the 345C series was fielded for 1933 but was little changed. It featured "No-Draft" ventilation on closed models, a vee'd radiator grille, and skirted fenders. Again, the 130- and 136-inch wheelbases were used and prices were lowered another $150. But in that worst of the

Depression years, LaSalle produced only 3381 cars.

The Depression had completely changed the industry's sales picture since LaSalle's introduction, and old marketing formulas no longer applied. When the car was conceived, the industry was still expanding, sales were strong, and new nameplates were in vogue. But the Depression meant retrenchment for all auto makers, including GM. One result was that the Pontiac, Olds, and Buick sales organizations were consolidated in 1933. LaSalle was given a careful review that year by company managers. They decided to discontinue the make after 1933—but they hadn't counted on the persuasiveness of one Harley Earl.

Earl went before a committee of top executives and told them he still had something to show them: Perhaps they would like to see what they were throwing away? He led them to the Art and Colour studio, and pulled back the drapes to

1932 Series 345B two-passenger convertible coupe

1932 Series 345B two-passenger coupe

1933 Series 345C five-passenger town sedan

1933 Series 345C five-passenger town coupe

1934 LaSalle Indianapolis 500 pace car (with Bill Rader)

1934 Series 350 five-passenger club sedan

reveal a stunning all-new model—slim-nosed and radically different. Warren Fitzgerald of GM styling asserted: "It can honestly be said that Harley Earl saved the LaSalle with his dramatic new design."

The 1934 Series 350 ushered in a new era for the make. In the lean Depression years, LaSalle had become too much like the standard Cadillac. Determined to achieve better sales, GM redefined the car and aimed it squarely at the medium-price field. The new '34 model was offered in just four Fleetwood body styles priced from $1495 to $1695, down over $700 from 1933. The previous, expensive ohv V-8 was replaced by an Oldsmobile-based L-head straight eight with aluminum pistons, five main bearings, and an automatic choke. It displaced 240.3 cubic inches (3.00 x 4.13 inches) and developed 95 bhp. Four-wheel hydraulic brakes, "Knee-Action" independent front suspension, ride control, and two-way hydraulic shocks were also part of the new package.

Earl's dramatic styling on the new 119-inch wheelbase was strikingly modern. Graceful pontoon fenders and a narrow grille formed a handsome front ensemble. The tall, slim radiator motif would serve as another trademark for the rest of LaSalle's production life. Distinguishing design details included double-bar bumpers with telescoping spring mounts, plus five pairs of hood portholes. The rear was curved in a gentle fastback and the spare tire was completely hidden. In tribute to its advanced design, the '34 LaSalle was selected as the pace car for the 1934 Indy 500. That season's sales total of 7128 units was not up to corporate expectations yet, but was still much better than in the previous two years.

For 1935, the LaSalle Series 35-50 sported Fisher's all-steel "Turret-Top" body on a one-inch longer (120-inch) wheelbase. Appearance

1936 Series 36-50 five-passenger touring sedan

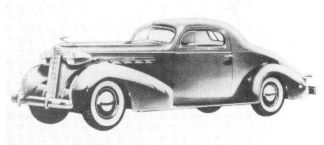
1936 Series 36-50 two-passenger coupe

1937 Series 37-50 two-door touring sedan

1937 Series 37-50 two-passenger coupe

1937 Series 37-50 convertible coupe

1937 Series 37-50 convertible sedan

changes included a cheaper single-bar bumper. The V-8 was stroked to 4.38 inches, which yielded 248 cid and 105 bhp. The clutch, gearbox, and rear axle were new. Moving further down-market, GM trimmed prices once more and the four-model lineup now ranged from $1255 to $1325. Sales improved to 8653 units, the highest since 1931. But again, management began to hesitate. In January, 1935, a financially desperate Packard had introduced its One-Twenty, which immediately became a strong competitor. Some 25,000 of these were built and sold, many to potential LaSalle buyers.

For 1936, the Series 36-50 carried different hood and grille styling. The frame was beefed up and the front doors were hinged at the front for greater safety. As a challenge to Packard, prices were lowered again to between $1175 and $1255, which represented an amazing value for money. The public responded: Over 13,000 LaSalles were built in '36. However, Packard built 55,000 One-Twentys that year, which also saw Ford field its own LaSalle competitor in the new Lincoln Zephyr.

By now, the overall market was on the way back and Cadillac upgraded the LaSalle for 1937. Again, it carried a V-8 (borrowed from the 1936 Cadillac Series 60), an L-head unit which displaced 322 cubic inches and developed 125 bhp on a 6.25:1 compression ratio. The engine mounts were softer, more flexible, yet quite stable—the forerunners of those used by most companies

soon afterward. LaSalle and Cadillac also pioneered the two-float carburetor, which helped prevent fuel starvation in sharp turns when the gas level shifted in the float bowl. An oil-bath air cleaner was another innovation that year, though other makes used it too. Underneath, LaSalle's new exhaust system carried a single large muffler instead of the former two small units. Suspension was improved by adding a torsional stabilizer bar at the front and a Panhard rod at the rear. Cadillac engineers discovered that using a torsion bar to tie the independently sprung front wheels together reduced oversteer.

The Series 37-50 rode on an enlarged 125-inch wheelbase. Its X-member frame was lowered 2.5 inches at the rear compared to the '36's, and the front floor was dropped 1.5 inches. Body styles included sedans, a coupe, a convertible coupe, and a convertible sedan, priced from $995 to $1485. More substantial styling was featured: A high beltline with a low roof and narrow side windows gave a sleek, elegant appearance. Better looks and lower prices pushed LaSalle production to a record 32,005 units, ahead of Lincoln Zephyr but still less than a third that of the small Packards, which now included a six-cylinder model.

LaSalle's 1937 sales record apparently satisfied GM, for the 1938 Series 38-50 was little changed. It featured a column gear lever, alligator-type hood, and a reworked grille and headlamp mountings. But 1938 was marked by an economic recession,

1937 Series 37-50 four-door touring sedan

Proposed 1941 LaSalle retained trademark grille styling.

1939 Series 39-50 convertible coupe

Fastback sedan was one of two '41 prototypes built.

and production skidded to 15,501—a lower total than Zephyr's and still less than a third the number of junior Packards that year.

There was a new body and revised styling for the 1939 LaSalle Series 39-50. Door sills were 1.75 inches lower and running boards were made optional. Glass area was increased by 27 percent giving the car a lighter, more modern look and better visibility. The dramatic new front end featured a narrow radiator grille no wider than a man's hand. The wheelbase was trimmed back to 120 inches and a sunroof option was announced. Rumble seats disappeared on LaSalle convertibles, replaced by small "opera seats" that folded against the bodysides. Mechanical changes included a new rear leaf-spring suspension and oil-saving piston rings. In a recovering national economy, 1939 production rose to 23,028 units—still trailing the small Packard but regaining the lead over Lincoln Zephyr.

Perhaps the best-remembered LaSalles were the last: the 1940 Series 50 and 52. The narrow vertical grille was retained, but headlights were now set in the fenders, and hood detailing was new. The Series 52 marked the high point in LaSalle styling. Wheelbase was increased to 123 inches and the V-8 now developed a healthy 130 bhp. (The power gain came by increasing the barrel diameters in the dual downdraft Carter carburetors by ⅛ of an inch.) The frame was heavier, the clutch smoother. A cross-link stabilizer was added from frame to rear axle which improved both ride and handling. Turn signal lights were standard. In contrast to the more conservative look of the Series 50, the 52 shared the "torpedo" lines of the highly successful Cadillac Series 62. At mid-year, a convertible coupe and sedan were added to the Series 52. Prices ranged from $1240 to $1895 in 1940 and model year production climbed to 24,133, compared to 90,000 small Packards and 22,000 Zephyrs.

But by that time, management had concluded Cadillac no longer needed a "companion car," especially since LaSalle was now infringing on Buick's price territory. There almost *was* a 1941 LaSalle: Prototypes were built, but the car was never produced. Instead, Cadillac revived its lower-priced Series 61 which partially filled the hole left by LaSalle's demise; the void was also partly filled by Buick.

It isn't hard to explain the failure of the 1927-33 LaSalle: The Depression gets the blame. After 1931, no expensive luxury car sold well and several great prestige makes disappeared because of this. But the poor showing of the 1934-40 LaSalle is harder to understand.

After 1935, the Packard One-Twenty and the Lincoln Zephyr vied with LaSalle for the same customer. Here, name had something to do with sales success: The small Packards and the Zephyr both carried the names of their prestigious parents, while LaSalle didn't. Also during the late '30s, Cadillac and LaSalle had grown more and more alike. By 1940, the LaSalle 52 and Cadillac 62 were nearly identical in form, finish, and performance, yet LaSalle was all too close to Buick in price. It didn't make sense to GM to continue LaSalle in what was a shrinking upper medium-price market.

From time to time there have been rumors of a LaSalle revival. The name and badge reappeared in 1955 on two GM Motorama showcars, a four-door hardtop and a two-seat convertible both named LaSalle II. Some early Corvair and Buick Riviera prototypes also wore LaSalle nameplates. More recently, the name was one of the frontrunners for Cadillac's compact sedan which bowed in 1975, but "Seville" finally won out.

The main reason for GM's reluctance to use the name is that, in some people's minds, it's associated with what might be called Cadillac's only failure. Christening the smaller 1975 Cadillac a LaSalle would have delighted three-quarters of the dealer body, as one division executive noted. "But it would alienate the other quarter." Among car enthusiasts, who would almost unanimously argue with that reasoning, LaSalle is a very respected marque: It built some of the finest automobiles in America before World War II. Car enthusiasts, however, are only an infinitesimal part of the new-car market. Therefore, it seems likely that the LaSalle name will never be resurrected for a future production model.

LaSalle II four-door hardtop at 1955 Motorama

1955 LaSalle II roadster—also strictly for show

The PENALTY OF LEADERSHIP

IN every field of human endeavor, he that is first must perpetually live in the white light of publicity. ¶Whether the leadership be vested in a man or in a manufactured product, emulation and envy are ever at work. ¶In art, in literature, in music, in industry, the reward and the punishment are always the same. ¶The reward is widespread recognition; the punishment, fierce denial and detraction. ¶When a man's work becomes a standard for the whole world, it also becomes a target for the shafts of the envious few. ¶If his work be merely mediocre, he will be left severely alone—if he achieve a masterpiece, it will set a million tongues a-wagging. ¶Jealousy does not protrude its forked tongue at the artist who produces a commonplace painting. ¶Whatsoever you write, or paint, or play, or sing, or build, no one will strive to surpass, or to slander you, unless your work be stamped with the seal of genius. ¶Long, long after a great work or a good work has been done, those who are disappointed or envious continue to cry out that it can not be done. ¶Spiteful little voices in the domain of art were raised against our own Whistler as a mountebank, long after the big world had acclaimed him its greatest artistic genius. ¶Multitudes flocked to Bayreuth to worship at the musical shrine of Wagner, while the little group of those whom he had dethroned and displaced argued angrily that he was no musician at all. ¶The little world continued to protest that Fulton could never build a steamboat, while the big world flocked to the river banks to see his boat steam by. ¶The leader is assailed because he is a leader, and the effort to equal him is merely added proof of that leadership. ¶Failing to equal or to excel, the follower seeks to depreciate and to destroy—but only confirms once more the superiority of that which he strives to supplant. ¶There is nothing new in this. ¶It is as old as the world and as old as the human passions—envy, fear, greed, ambition, and the desire to surpass. ¶And it all avails nothing. ¶If the leader truly leads, he remains—the leader. ¶Master-poet, master-painter, master-workman, each in his turn is assailed, and each holds his laurels through the ages. ¶That which is good or great makes itself known, no matter how loud the clamor of denial. ¶That which deserves to live—lives.

Cadillac Motor Car Co. Detroit, Mich.

A leader in automotive innovation, Cadillac also pioneered new approaches to automobile advertising. This 1914 piece, written by Theodore MacManus, is one of the most famous of all. It captures the essence of Cadillac's dedication to excellence.

SPOTLIGHT:
Cadillac and LaSalle Mascots

Over the years, the style of Cadillac and LaSalle radiator ornamentation has generally followed contemporary design trends, except for cars like Mercedes-Benz and Rolls-Royce which retain their classic radiator shells even today. Starting in the mid 1920s, craftsmen fashioned traditional type mascots for Cadillac and LaSalle, using coat of arms heraldry for the former and an explorer motif for the latter. Both designs prevailed until the end of the 1930 model year, when the mascots gave way to more modern figures influenced by the art deco movement, which was beginning to dominate industrial design worldwide.

It is necessary to point out that mascots were originally deluxe accessories offered at extra cost. And they weren't especially cheap. Since they were not fitted to every car which left the factory, the early mascots are quite scarce today.

For its new 1930 V-8 models, Cadillac designed a rather lovely goddess in the art deco mode. She leans far forward into the wind, with hair and scarf flowing gracefully behind her. This was the first in a long series of goddesses which would adorn Cadillac hoods through the late '50s, when all resemblance to human form disappeared. For the first couple of years in the '30s, LaSalle shared the Cadillac goddess.

An alternate design was also available. This was the graceful heron, certainly patterned after the stork used on the Hispano-Suiza, the car which inspired the original LaSalle's body design. The heron was quite stylized; it appeared in two distinct renditions for both Cadillac and LaSalle, and lasted until 1933. Beginning with its all-new 1934 LaSalle, Cadillac adopted a series of bullets or bombs, influenced perhaps by the "futuristic" mascots of Jan and Joel Martel, Parisian designers of the 1920s. Such streamlined shapes were in keeping with Harley Earl's aerodynamic body styling for the 1934 model.

A little-known fact is that the finely molded goddess of 1941 remained in Cadillac accessory books through the mid '50s. Many enthusiasts believe that later models fitted with this ornament are blatantly "non-stock," but in fact the goddess was available over the counter until 1956 at least. The 1957 Cadillac adopted a finned ornament, which effectively prevented the '41 mascot from being attached, except perhaps with an Erector set.

In 1971, Cadillac introduced a modern form of mascot for the Eldorado line—an upright full-color crest surrounded by a laurel wreath. This is still offered on Cadillac's senior models. Perhaps these are not true mascots in the usual sense. But they do provide a distinctive touch for what would otherwise be a featureless expanse of metal. Spring loaded for safety, they are harmless to pedestrians and help some drivers place the car in traffic. In a way, mascots have now come full circle, and are again very popular today.

Rene Robert Cavalier, Sieur de la Salle, stands on a base which depicts a campfire, an axe, and a broken canoe paddle. The French explorer, with his hat held out, was jokingly said to be taking up a collection so he could buy a Cadillac. This rare mascot, introduced with the first LaSalle in 1927, was made of pewter and was nickel-plated until 1928, after which chrome plating was used. It was available through 1930.

The LaSalle mascot of 1934 was the first in a long line of similarly designed hood ornaments which evolved into a finned bullet or bomb. It was used until the end of LaSalle production in 1940.

The famous herald, first in a line of Cadillac mascots, was introduced in 1926 and was offered through 1930. Silver plate was used in 1926-27, while later examples were chromed. The crest on the herald's tunic is a full-color gold-plated cloisonne. An inscription on the base tells us these mascots were made in Chicago, but nothing more of their origins is known.

This example of the beautiful Cadillac and LaSalle heron was found on 1930 through early 1932 models. It was made of chrome-plated brass. Late in 1932, the metal was changed to die-cast zinc, which necessitated a shorter and thicker neck for greater strength. The heron was available on both Cadillac and LaSalle from 1930-33. In 1933, the design was simplified and all traces of detail in the wings and tail were removed. The result was a smoothly formed, highly stylized creature.

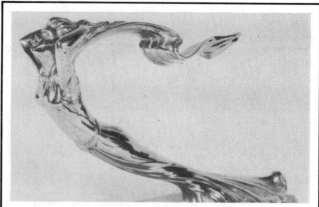

Made of die-cast zinc, this sleek Cadillac-LaSalle goddess of 1930-32 is a scarce item today and highly sought-after. These mascots were manufactured, like all Cadillac-LaSalle ornaments after 1930, by Ternstedt of Detroit. A rumor persists that the goddesses used on the Cadillac V-16s were larger than those on the V-8 and V-12 models, but this is not true: One size fit all.

In 1933 and '34, the goddess was simplified along the same lines as the heron. While there is still some detail in the hair and face, the balance of the form was streamlined to match the more streamlined lines of the 1933 models. This particular figure was used on V-8 cars only.

This goddess adorned the 1933-36 V-12 and V-16 cars. A slightly larger mascot was used on these models, although it was also available for V-8s on special order. The immense size of the V-16 and V-12 probably justified a larger figurehead than that of the V-8. This goddess was chrome-plated as standard, but could be gold-plated at extra cost.

The 1935-36 goddess for V-8 cars is considered by many knowledgeable enthusiasts to be the biggest clunker of them all. All detail and grace are gone in this rather heavy chunk of die-cast metal.

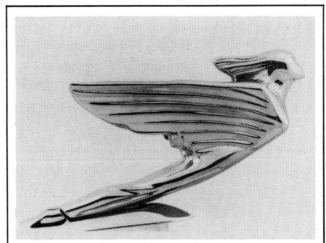

For its new V-16 in 1937, Cadillac designed a new mascot. It stands more upright than its V-8 sister, but lacks the glass wing. This hood ornament was retained through the end of the V-16s in 1940.

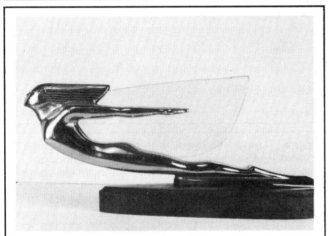

With introduction of the 1936 models, the first glass wing appeared on the V-8 mascot. The profile is lower and longer than its predecessor, which added to the appeal. There is little artful detail except for the hair. This same goddess also appeared on the 1938 V-12.

In 1939, the goddess was stretched out to full length for the first time and would remain so until these flying ladies disappeared in the '50s. The last year for the glass wing was 1940. This ornament doubled as an upward-pivoting handle to open the hood.

In 1941, there was a return to detail and the goddess again had a face. This ornament, like the 1939-40 version, was used to open the hood.

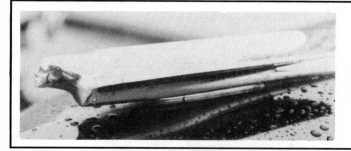

This 1942 ornament set the style for the rest of the Cadillac goddesses. The same general design was utilized, with variations in length or width of the wings, until the mid '50s when it was discontinued.

The wreath and crest of the Eldorado was introduced in 1971, and is used today on all senior models. The wreath is chrome, while the crest is of full-color acrylic.

The Cadillac Crest

The famous Cadillac coat of arms, which was registered as a trademark on August 6, 1906, is a familiar symbol though few have paused to wonder about its meaning. Cadillac itself has published several explanations over the years, from which the following account is taken.

In the language of ancient heraldry, the coat of arms is described like this: "Quarterly, the first and fourth gold, a fess sable between three merlettes of the same, posed two in chief and one in base. Second and third gules quartering argent, three bars azure." Translated literally, this means: a quartered shield; the upper left and lower right corners gold, containing black bands, with two duck-like birds above and one below the band; the upper right and lower left corners containing two red quarters, and two silver quarters with blue bars.

Cadillac goes on to explain that the coronet, or "couronne," represented the "six ancient counts of France." Interestingly, the original de la Mothe Cadillac arms and the trademark, filed in 1906, have seven round points or pearls, as does the crest currently used. This may have been done for artistic purposes. Over the years, the crest has appeared with as many as 18 points but no fewer than seven.

The first and fourth quarters represent the arms de la Mothe, continues the Cadillac description. The birds or "merlettes" are heraldic adaptations of the martin, but are shown without legs or beaks. The ancient historian Guillame commented that merlettes are "given for a difference, to younger brothers to put them in mind that in order to raise themselves they are to look to the wings of virtue and merit and not to the legs, having but little land to set their feet on." The second and third quarters were added to the de la Mothe arms after "a favorable marriage increased their estates," according to the Cadillac explanation. The red stands for "prowess and boldness in action," the silver for "purity, charity, virtue, and plenty," and the blue for "knightly valor."

Color photography page 33, bottom, and pages 34 through 40 by Bud Juneau. Our special thanks to the owners of these showcase Cadillacs: Charles Jones (Madam X V-16); Allan Jones (1938 V-16 Formal Sedan); Jim Bowersox (1941 62 Coupe and 1948 60 Special); Bob Brelsford (1947 62 Sedanet); and Dale Hall (1949 62 Sedan). All other photos courtesy Cadillac Motor Car Division.

Cadillac
COLOR SHOWCASE I

Top: LaSalle Mascot, 1927-30
Center: 1927 LaSalle Series 303 Convertible
Bottom: 1928 Series 341A Dual-Cowl Phaeton

Top: 1930 Series 452 Madam X V-16 Sedan
Bottom: 1938 Series 90 V-16 Formal Sedan

Top: 1941 Series 60 Special Fleetwood
Bottom: 1941 Series 62 Coupe

Top: 1947 Series 62 Sedanet
Bottom: 1948 Series 60 Special Fleetwood

Top: 1949 Series 62 Sedan
Bottom: 1949 Series 62 Sedan

Top: 1952 Series 62 Convertible
Bottom: Series 62 Convertible show car, 1952

Top: LeMans show car, 1953
Bottom: 1954 Eldorado

La Espada

Top: 1955 60 Special Sedan
Bottom: La Espada show car, 1954

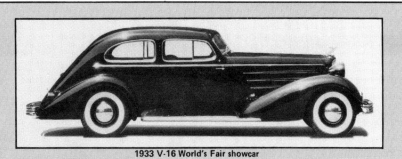
1933 V-16 World's Fair showcar

"A Standard for the Whole World" 1930-1942

There was very little difference between the 1930 Cadillac V-8 and the previous year's model. The most significant change for the company was in total sales: 7000 fewer cars were sold in 1930 than in 1929. But Cadillac continued to give its buyers wide variety. The V-8 line offered a choice of seven Fisher and 14 semi-custom Fleetwood bodies—not counting coachwork available on the V-16 and LaSalle chassis. The V-8 engine used a three-piece block with an aluminum crankcase which had two cast-iron cylinder barrels bolted to it. It was a heavy, complicated design so production costs were high, but it would be continued through 1933. The 1930 V-8 developed 95 bhp and the transmission was semi-synchromesh that season. All V-8 Cadillacs rode on a 140-inch wheelbase. Prices remained high. A four-door convertible with Fleetwood coachwork, called the "Fleetway All-Weather phaeton," listed for $4700.

Styling for 1931 did not change much. The hood now had five vertical doors on each side instead of louvers, but wheelbase shrank by half a foot to 134 inches. Horsepower and engine specifications stayed the same. Wheel diameter remained 19 inches, but tire size was reduced and optional

18-inch wheels were offered. Prices were not cut in an effort to stem declining sales. So, sales kept sliding, despite attractive, easy time payments offered by that pioneer of auto installment purchasing, General Motors Acceptance Corporation (GMAC).

Cadillac had good styling though, and the division stayed with it. Its practice of offering a mind-boggling variety of body styles and options continued throughout the early '30s. "Hard times," of course, plagued all luxury car manufacturers, but Cadillac was not the least fortunate of these. While Packard and Lincoln would depend on middle-priced models to stay afloat, Pierce-Arrow and Franklin both ceased production during the Depression era. Had Cadillac been an independent like Pierce-Arrow, its fate might have been the same. But as part of the vast, financially solid GM empire, Cadillac survived partly by continuing profits earned by other divisions, Chevrolet in particular. And remember, General Motors never lost money in those years, contrary to popular belief.

The 1932 Cadillac was a completely fresh design and had many new features. The body and fender lines were now much smoother and more rounded than before; the fenders flared out more,

1930 Series 353 five-passenger sedan

1931 Series 355 five-passenger coupe

and blended gracefully into curved running boards. Aesthetically, the new smaller wheels made the car appear lower and slimmer, a look accentuated by parking lights and dual-beam headlamps mounted in bullet-shaped housings. The dashboard layout was new, and on closed models all doors could be locked from the inside. The usual plethora of body styles was offered, but 1933 would be the last year for the dashing roadster model.

There were a number of mechanical innovations for 1932. The V-8's horsepower was increased to 115 bhp via redesigned intake manifolds, and its cast-iron pistons were now tin plated. The differential and front end were both lighter, and adjustable shock absorbers were introduced. The transmission got helical-cut gears for "silent" shifting, and could be equipped with the optional vacuum-operated clutch. Among the options were full chrome wheel discs to cover the wire wheels, as well as hot water or air heaters priced at $27.50 and $34.50, respectively.

Despite this fine model line and many improvements, Cadillac's sales outlook remained gloomy. Less than 3000 V-8s were sold in 1932, a drastic drop from '31 when 11,000 units found customers. Things were even worse in 1933, with V-8 sales bottoming out at around 2100 cars.

Ironically, Cadillacs kept getting better throughout this bleak period. New styling for 1933 made them among the handsomest cars on the road. The design was very fluid now. The horizontal hood doors were accented by chrome speed streaks. The radiator shell was V-shaped and painted to match body color. The horns and headlight brackets were combined as single units. Fenders were skirted, and complemented the smooth body lines. Windshields on closed cars were one-piece fixed units. In previous years, they were hinged at the top and could be opened from the bottom for ventilation, but there was no need for this in 1933 thanks to introduction of GM's "No-Draft" ventilation. This consisted of a cowl vent through which fresh air was ducted into the interior and swivelling vent windows in the front doors. There were 16 bodies to choose from, available on either the V-8 or V-12 chassis, supplied as before by Fisher and Fleetwood. The V-8 cars also gained vacuum-operated brakes previously available on the larger-engined cars only. There were no changes in tire size or horsepower.

But changes had to be made if Cadillac was to survive. GM knew it had to reduce the number of parts unique to each division and cut corners elsewhere by whatever means necessary. To put Cadillac back on the road to success, Nicholas Dreystadt was brought in as division general manager in 1934. It was Dreystadt's management that helped restore Cadillac, making it "a Standard for the Whole World" and the nation's dominant luxury automobile.

The 1934 line was extensively modified with new styling by Harley Earl. Three wheelbase lengths were offered: 128, 136, and 146 inches. The smallest Series 10 shared its Fisher body with the Buick line. A magnificent show car on the V-16 chassis, exhibited at the Chicago World's Fair in 1933, had set the style for the '34 models. It was

1932 Series 355B five-passenger all-weather phaeton

1932 Series 355B two-passenger coupe

1933 Series 355C two-passenger convertible coupe

1933 Series 355C Fleetwood seven-passenger sedan

designed by the Art & Colour Studio and dubbed the "Aerodynamic Coupe" by Cadillac. As one of the first closed cars with fastback lines, it made styling history. Several similar fastbacks were built to special order on V-8 chassis between 1934 and 1937.

Styling features of the production '34 models

1933 V-16 World's Fair showcar

1934 Series 355D five-passenger convertible sedan

1934 Series 355D convertible coupe

1935 Series 10 five-passenger town coupe

included "pontoon" front fenders accented by beautiful, thin, dual-blade bumpers (inspired by the wings of the biplane) mounted on coil springs to absorb impact. The horns were concealed under the hood. Bodies and windshields were four inches wider than in 1933. On some models the external spare tire was relocated inside the trunk for the first time.

But the big news in 1934 was mechanical. The brilliant Maurice Olley had engineered a new independent front suspension for all GM cars. The company called it "Knee-Action," and it made automotive headlines. The suspension change resulted in a redesigned chassis with the engine moved eight inches further forward so it was cradled between the independent front axles. This meant the passenger compartment could be longer with no increase in wheelbase. There was also a new steering mechanism, and a rear torsion bar was added for a more stable ride. An X-member frame and Hotchkiss drive provided a lower floor tunnel. Pushbutton starting was also new and there was more legroom for the driver because the parking brake handle was relocated to a position under the dashboard. The 1934 V-8 engine had dual valve springs for the first time plus a redesigned crankshaft, Lynite aluminum pistons, and higher compression. Horsepower increased to 118 bhp and a semi-automatic choke helped improve gas mileage. The public responded well to this new package: Cadillac's sales decline was reversed.

After the massive changes made in 1934, the division fielded a very similar line the following year. The expensive-to-build "biplane" bumpers, however, were replaced by a more conventional single-blade design. A stabilizer bar was added to the front suspension, and the V-8's compression was reduced.

Cadillac ordained a facelift and a completely new V-8 for its 1936 models which came in three series, the 60, 70, and 75. Closed bodies now featured GM's all-steel "Turret Top" construction. The division was now recovering rapidly. GM had learned a lot about production economies and especially component sharing among its various divisions, so all its lines were now somewhat similar to each other. But Cadillac's stylists and engineers were the best in the industry, and other GM makes would benefit from their talent.

The big news for '36 was the "monobloc" V-8, development of which had started in 1932. This smooth, quiet, and strong powerplant would be retained without major changes through 1948. It also hastened the departure of the V-12, which it rendered virtually obsolete. With its porcelain-coated exhaust manifolds and one-piece cast-iron block, the new V-8 was a lively engine that gave excellent service. Hydraulic valve-lifters located down in the block started an engineering trend which can still be seen in present-day engines.

1936 Fleetwood Series 75 town sedan

1936 Fleetwood Series 70 convertible sedan

1937 Fleetwood Series 70 coupe

1937 Fleetwood Series 75 convertible sedan

1937 Fleetwood Series 70 convertible coupe

1937 Series 85 town cabriolet

Also in '36, Cadillac introduced hydraulic brakes, which were doubly effective since the V-8 cars were lighter than before. The frame was more rigid and the front suspension refined. Though narrower, the 1936 radiator provided 10 percent better cooling than past designs. Accordingly, the grille became narrower, too. This was also the first year for the divided "V" windshield.

The 1936 Series 60, on a 121-inch wheelbase, shared its body with the smaller Buick and Oldsmobile and was the lowest-priced Cadillac since 1908. At the other end of the scale, the Fleetwood Series 70 (131-inch wheelbase) and Series 75 (138-inch) offered a total of 14 body styles. Cadillac quality and craftsmanship were at their peak in this period before World War II. Every car was powerful yet highly refined.

The 1937 models, introduced in October, 1936, featured a restyled radiator and hood area. Interiors were fancier and more luxurious compared to the more austere look of prior years. The new models weighed about 250 pounds less than the '36s. Most of that was trimmed from the engine and transmission including the cylinder head and flywheel, yet the V-8 block was actually beefed up for strength. A new Stromberg carburetor with fully automatic choke was adopted and all V-8 models now shared the same engine displacement. (The 1936 Series 60 engine had a smaller capacity than that of upper-series cars.)

With its larger engine, the 1937 Series 60 was a real performer. It continued to share its basic body structure with Buick, though the 60's wheelbase was longer this year at 124 inches. This model sold in the upper medium-price class just above LaSalle. The rest of the '37 lineup comprised the Series 65, offered only as a Fisher-built sedan; and the Series 70 and 75, available with Fleetwood bodies on 131- and 138-inch wheelbases.

1938 Series 75 convertible coupe

1938 Series 75 convertible sedan

1938 Series 65 seven-passenger touring sedan

1938 Series 60 five-passenger touring sedan

1938 Series 60 Special touring sedan

1939 Series 75 convertible coupe

Styling was the byword for 1938. From the drawing board of young William Mitchell came a new model, the 60 Special sedan. It made almost everything else on the road look old-fashioned and influenced automotive design for a generation. The 60 Special was an entirely new concept—the total car. It was long and low, and eschewed running boards. Its trunk blended smoothly into the main body. Radically slim roof pillars allowed doors and windshield to be wider than on any other car in the class, providing superior visibility. Instead of the traditional bulky upper door frames there were thin-but-strong bright metal frames which gave the car a sort of convertible look. With its combination of high style and sound engineering the 60 Special outsold all other V-8 Cadillacs, even though 1938 was a recession year and overall industry sales were down markedly.

New styling was also applied to the rest of the line, and the Series 70 was eliminated. The V-8 models now offered more interior room thanks to longer wheelbases and a new chassis design which lowered the entire car. Prices ranged from $1695 for the Series 60 to $5115 for the V-8 Series 75 on a 141-inch wheelbase. Radiator grilles grew wider and hoods more massive—an abrupt change from the narrow frontispieces of 1936-37. Fenders were wider, and tapered headlamps were moved to a lower position between fender and grille housing. The hood was hinged at the rear for the first time. Dashboards and interiors were revamped throughout the line. Hypoid final drive, repositioned springs, a flywheel hub-damper, and column-mounted gearshift were among the year's new mechanical features.

An improving economy meant higher sales in 1939, a year in which pointed noses reappeared on GM cars. The new styling featured a three-element front-end treatment with a central

1940 Fleetwood Series 72 Sedan

1940 Series 62 convertible sedan

1940 Fleetwood Series 72 five-passenger formal sedan

All the comforts of home in the 1940 Series 75

radiator grille flanked either side by "catwalk" grilles in the area between the fender and the main nose section, just below the headlamps. The Series 61 replaced the 60 and the 60 Special became a separate model. The new 61 picked up many of the 60 Special's styling touches: Windows and windshield were deep and its windows were framed in bright metal. Like the Special, the 61 offered optional running boards and a sliding sunroof. All 1939 Cadillacs got a newly designed dashboard, an optional vacuum-operated power antenna, rubber protectors on the rear fenders, and a feature called "Controlled-Action Ride." The latter referred basically to the higher rear axle rotation center which improved passenger comfort. License plate brackets were relocated to the center of the trunk lid. The rumble-seat convertible of past years went the way of the wind.

The 1940 models were mostly unchanged in appearance. Grille bars were wider, and parking lights surfaced at the tops of the front fenders. Directional signals became standard as did sealed-beam headlights. The Series 62 replaced the 61 and offered two new "torpedo" body styles fresh from the Art & Colour studios, a sedan and a five-passenger coupe. The Series 72 made its debut as a smaller version of the big 75, and featured a new recirculating-ball steering system. This was the last year in which the 75 was available with a full range of body styles. Though this series was continued until 1976, it was generally available only as a limousine or long-wheelbase sedan after 1940.

The all-new 1941 models genuinely established Cadillac as America's ultimate automotive status symbol. Fastidious styling was derived from Mitchell's 1938 60 Special but had deft improvements, and set a trend that would be followed by the rest of the industry in short order. These cars reeked class. They were so well designed that even their heavy use of chrome did not seem at all garish or inappropriate.

The durable V-8 was unchanged for '41, but the frame was redesigned to be much more rigid for a smoother ride on all types of roads. The model lineup was shuffled: The one-year-old Series 72 was dropped, the 61 reappeared, and a new Series 67 designation was invented. All models featured the "torpedo" bodyshell which had originated in concept with the first 60 Special. Headlamps were mounted in, rather than on top of, the front fenders. There was a new horizontal egg-crate grille which later would be widely imitated. All four fenders had squared-off trailing edges yet harmonized nicely with the torpedo's rounded contours. Emblems and trim were finished to jewel-like perfection. Accessories abounded: Radios, fender skirts, driving lights, mirrors, windshield washer, back-up lights, and Hydra-Matic transmission were all available. It was a banner year: Sales met all expectations as Cadillac sold

19,000 more cars than in 1940.

Production of the restyled 1942 Cadillacs lasted only a few months before the division turned to defense work. Less than 5000 cars were built for the model year, though the design would be carried over with few changes for 1946-47. It was a preview of things to come. Bodies were more streamlined: Front fenders flowed back deeply into the front doors and were now teardrop-shaped; rear fenders repeated the same theme. The fastback look which had captivated America was strongly emphasized. Only the Series 75 retained a more upright, four-square shape.

From the depths of the early '30s to America's entry into World War II, confident managers and talented engineers had led Cadillac to new heights. The marque had become the standard of comparison for luxury-car buyers. After a distinguished wartime role building tanks, aircraft engines, and munitions, Cadillac would be stronger than ever before in its history and ready to face the postwar world.

1941 Series 62 convertible sedan

1941 Series 62 convertible

1942 Series 62 five-passenger sedan

Spacious elegance—the 1942 Series 67 sedan

1942 Fleetwood Series 60 Special sedan

1942 Series 62 five-passenger coupe

SPOTLIGHT: The 60 Special

Young William Mitchell styled this pace-setting automobile as his first assignment from Harley Earl. The work began in January, 1936. The result, announced less than two years later, was a milestone in automotive design with features that would be copied by the rest of GM—and the industry—in short order.

At a time when most cars used headlight shells at-

The 1938 60 Special (above) and the 1939 edition (below)

tached to the hood—even other Cadillacs still had this—the 60 Special's fender-mounted headlight shells were something of a sensation. So was its lack of traditional running boards. Remember, this was 1938 and nobody had *ever* seen a shape like the 60 Special's. Its faired-in trunk, thin door posts, and chrome-banded window frames were all completely new. There

wasn't a single detail out of place: Nothing was left to chance.

The original design evolved over four model years and as time went on, it seemed to get better and better. For 1939 came a more delicate grille and "catwalk" fender vents. The grillework became more pronounced in 1940. For 1941, Mitchell created the distinctive egg-crate grille style

that would endure for a generation. Town cars and formal sedans were offered, along with an optional sliding sunroof.

After 1941, 60 Special styling was more closely related to the rest of the Cadillac line. But the car had won such a place in the hearts of buyers that its design influence can still be seen in today's Fleetwood Brougham.

The 1940 town car model (above) and the restyled 1941 60 Special (below)

"The Reward Is Widespread Recognition" 1946-1956

A glimpse inside the Cadillac styling studio, circa 1946

In the famous "The Penalty of Leadership" advertisement, Theodore MacManus wrote, "That which is good or great makes itself known, no matter how loud the clamor of denial." This particular line could be carved in granite as a monument to Cadillac's success. For years, the automotive press has commented that Mercedes-Benz has the best-engineered cars, Rolls-Royce the best finished, Lincoln the most carefully constructed. Yet mention the word "luxury" to most Americans, and the car that immediately springs to mind is Cadillac. That's been especially true for the years after World War II.

In 1947, Cadillac passed Packard in calendar year production for the first time since 1934. This was significant, because Packard was building several models priced quite a bit less than the cheapest Cadillac, and should have stayed ahead. Packard did overtake its old rival in 1948 and 1949, but Cadillac moved ahead to stay in 1950. That was the first year the division built over 100,000 cars. Since then, Cadillac supremacy in the luxury field hasn't been seriously challenged.

The early postwar Cadillacs, like those which came before, broke a lot of new ground in both styling and engineering. The most significant accomplishments appeared in 1948, the year of the tailfin, and in 1949, the first year for the overhead-valve V-8. Though later Cadillacs have since joined the '48s and '49s on the collector's "must" list, these two models are among the most desirable of all—and for several good reasons.

1946 Series 62 sedan

1947 Series 62 convertible

1948 Fleetwood Series 60 Special sedan (not production)

1948 Series 62 convertible

These two design breakthroughs did not appear immediately after the war. Like other car makers who had switched to producing wartime materiel after Pearl Harbor, Cadillac had only its 1942 tooling available when hostilities ended. This was pressed into service again in late 1945. The resulting 1946 models were powered by the well-proven 346-cid L-head engine and offered Hydra-Matic transmission as an option. One major styling change from 1942 was a bolt-on alteration: full wraparound bumpers, instead of the truncated ones that stopped at the outer edges of the front end. Also, rectangular parking lights replaced the round 1942 units. Seven different body styles were offered on four different wheelbases. The 60 Special, with its graceful styling which had made such a hit before the war, continued to be the highest-priced Cadillac, except for the long-wheelbase 75. Both these models used Fleetwood bodies, lavishly fitted out and finished with impeccable craftsmanship.

In the abbreviated production run for calendar year 1945, Cadillac built only 1142 cars. Calendar 1946 production went up to 28,000 units as the division felt the strain of pent-up public demand for new postwar cars. Over 100,000 orders were on the books by the time the factory switched to the mostly carryover 1947 models.

Minor changes were made to distinguish the '47s from the '46s. A winged trunk insignia replaced the previous "V," there were now full wheel covers, and new upholstery and paint combinations were offered. The model lineup was almost a rerun of 1946. Production now began to hit full stride: By the end of the year, Cadillac had

built nearly 60,000 cars. The 1947 line continued with the 150-bhp 346-cid L-head engine.

Of course, the 1946-47 models were a mere prelude to the potent one-two punch that followed: a styling tour de force and an engineering triumph. In 1948, Cadillac set an industry styling trend which lasted 15 years. In 1949, it unveiled the first modern short-stroke overhead-valve V-8, an engine others would soon copy.

Most car enthusiasts are aware that the tailfin of the 1948 Cadillac was inspired by the Lockheed P-38 "Lightning" pursuit fighter of World War II. But fewer know this particular aircraft also inspired other features found in the early postwar Cadillacs and other GM products. Still fewer realize that the 1948 Cadillac began a styling tradition which has endured far longer than the fin, and is still found on some 1980 models: the distinctive Cadillac grille.

For many years, car stylists had been fascinated by the design elements of certain airplanes. Some of these inspired various automobile styling themes. The P-38 was a particularly beautiful aircraft, and Harley Earl was quite taken with it. Earl and his staff got their first look at one in 1939 when they were allowed to examine the then-secret plane at the Detroit Army Airfield. Back at the studio, Earl set his men to work on some ⅜th-scale models which incorporated dozens of ideas adapted from the Lockheed. Among these were the now-familiar peaked rear fender tips, patterned after the P-38's twin tail. The plane also influenced the front-end design in some of these models which carried bulbous, bullet-like noses and pontoon-style front fenders. Even the windshields resembled those of the P-38, with some having a wraparound design which foreshadowed 1954-55 GM production cars. The engine air scoops of the P-38 found their way onto the 'Futuramic' 1948-49 Oldsmobiles. As styling work proceeded for the '48 Cadillac, the bullet noses and pontoon fenders of the earlier studies gradually faded into more conventional shapes. However, the tailfins, at first debated by management, were ultimately retained.

Harley Earl, speaking of Cadillac's design philosophy, once said: "A fundamental we have learned . . . is not to step too far at a time; but every now and again we take a risk." The tailfin was indeed a risk, but it had a good rationale. Earl found one of his main design problems was to overcome the complaint that the 1942-47 Cadillacs looked too much like lesser GM products, Buick and Oldsmobile in particular. "We wanted to give the car some definition, especially at the rear, which had been greatly neglected by most contemporary designs," Earl said. (This search for individual "brand-name" identity is what gave Buick its famous "portholes" and sweep-spear side treatment in 1949, and Pontiac its prewar "Silver Streak" hood and deck trim, which was further emphasized on postwar models.)

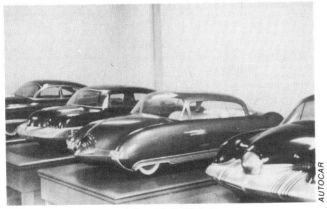

Early postwar clay models with P-38 influence

AUTOCAR

Full-size Coupe deVille rendering in Cadillac styling studio

The front end of the 1948 Cadillac introduced a more lasting design theme: a full-width grille with a raised center section. On the '48s, it was a simple cross-hatched affair; later it became the gaudy, heavily chromed "dollar grin" derisively chided by English commentators (who never bothered to measure the square inches of chrome on the front of a Rolls-Royce). This trademark grille theme remained even after the tailfins had melted away in the early '60s, and is still found on the DeVilles of 1980. It was a touch that seemed right for the car, and remains one of Cadillac's nicest styling traditions.

The 60 Special for 1948 continued its own tradition as it was still offered only as a sedan on an exclusive 133-inch wheelbase. As before, it shared the Fleetwood designation with the Series 75. The latter was originally scheduled to have the same all-new look as the rest of the '48 line, but the need to amortize prewar dies in this low-volume series caused the division to continue with the older body styling until 1950.

Sharing the 60 Special's new lines were the 126-inch-wheelbase 61 and 62 series, each of which offered a magnificent two-door fastback body style nicknamed the "sedanet." Many observers in and out of GM say this superlative body style (also used by the firm's lesser makes) was one of the industry's all-time design greats. Indeed, the grandly praised Bentley Continental, which appeared in 1952, had body styling not unlike that of the Cadillac sedanet. Also offered in the 62 series were a four-door sedan and convertible coupe (the latter with standard electric window lifts). The 61 series, which sold for about $175 less than the 62, was limited to the sedan and sedanet only. The 61's lower price was achieved by using slightly less elaborate trim and upholstery.

The instrument panel design adopted for all 1948 models grouped all dials directly ahead of the driver in a protruding "drum" or pod. (This was abandoned in favor of a less costly, flat, hooded panel for 1949). The dash flowed down smoothly and ended just above the carpeted floor. Ducts were built into the front doors, through which warm air from the defroster circulated to the side windows as well as the windshield.

The basic 1948 design was carried over for 1949 with only a more glittery grille as the main distinguishing feature. A significant new body style debuted that year, the pretty, pillarless Series 62 Coupe deVille. Together with Buick's Riviera and Oldsmobile's Holiday, this car has the distinction of being the first volume-produced hardtop in the American industry. One experimental Coupe deVille was built on the long 60 Special wheelbase, but it never went into production.

There was no doubt Cadillac had blitzed the high-priced field with its 1948 styling, but few outside of GM expected the division to fire another

Ernest Seaholm (right) with Ed Cole

The 1949 overhead-valve 331-cid V-8

revolutionary salvo in 1949. This was the all-new V-8 engine which had been evolving since before 1936, when a replacement for the long-running L-head V-8 was first contemplated. By the early '40s, the L-head design had reached the limits of its compression, and since much higher octane gasoline was expected to be commercially available after the war, a new V-8 was needed to take advantage of this. By the week before Pearl Harbor, experimental engines were already being tested, but the war effort delayed introduction of the new engine until 1949.

The engine development program was in competent hands. It involved chief engineer John F. Gordon, who succeeded Ernest Seaholm in 1943 and became division general manager in 1946; Harry F. Barr, later GM vice-president for Engineering; and Edward N. Cole, who replaced Gordon as chief engineer in 1946, and later became GM president.

The design goals for the new engine were simple: a compression ratio of 7:1 or less for export, adjustable to as high as 12:1 for the domestic market; good fuel economy; smooth performance; lightness; longevity; clean design; and optimum serviceability. All these requirements were achieved, though it took time to do so. "It is doubtful if any engine has ever had a more thorough testing," the engineers wrote in 1949. "The engine in its final form was run well over 1,000,000 miles before the first 1949 Cadillac was made public. Between 1946 and 1948 more than 25 engines were built and subjected to the most strenuous tests...One experimental and one production 1949 engine were run for more than 100 hours at 4250 rpm with wide-open throttle... there was no appreciable wear."

Early plans called for the new V-8 to have a 309 cubic-inch capacity. However, when word got out about Oldsmobile's new 307-cid unit—developed separately from Cadillac's but at about the same time—the division's engineers upped displacement to 331 cid for a size difference more appropriate for a luxury make. Bore and stroke were 3.81 x 3.63 inches—very modern, oversquare dimensions. In operation, the new V-8 was absolutely smooth at all speeds, thanks to a five-main-bearing crankshaft. It was smaller in every dimension than the 346 and weighed 188 pounds less, yet it developed 160 bhp, seven percent more horsepower than its predecessor. Compared to its sister Olds V-8, the 331 had 10 percent more displacement but cranked out 18.5 percent more horsepower and weighed a few pounds less. It made every Cadillac a 100-plus mph car.

Though never looked upon as racing machines, Cadillacs of this period had extraordinary performance. The 1950 Series 61 was relatively light, and when equipped with the 160-hp V-8, stick-shift, and 3.77 rear-axle ratio, was the fastest passenger car in the United States, according to

1951 Series 62 convertible

several authorities. "I owned one of these and a new Jaguar XK-120," said racing driver Edward Gaylord, who later built the unsuccessful Gaylord luxury car. "The Cadillac was the faster car up to about 90 mph...The only competition I had in acceleration was from the small 135-hp Olds 88 coupe, but the Cadillac engine was substantially more efficient both in performance and economy." On the international circuit, Briggs Cunningham campaigned a near-stock Coupe deVille and a Cadillac-powered specially bodied car at Le Mans in 1950. He finished 10th and 11th overall; the Coupe deVille actually came in *ahead* of the special.

Styling didn't change much at Cadillac in the early '50s. According to Bill Mitchell, who was a rising young designer in the Art and Colour Studio at the time, a traditional Cadillac look was always retained from year to year: "If a grille is changed, the tail end is left alone; if a fin is changed, the

1949 Series 61 "sedanet" five-passenger coupe

1950 Series 61 sedan

The shape of Cadillac's future as seen in late 1949

1951 Fleetwood Series 60 Special sedan

1952 Series 62 convertible

1952 Series 62 sedan

1953 Eldorado convertible

1953 Fleetwood Series 60 Special sedan

grille is not monkeyed with." Through 1953, the changes were in detail only: a one-piece windshield in 1950, small auxiliary grilles under the headlamps in 1951, a winged badge in that spot for 1952, "Dagmar" bumpers and a one-piece backlight in 1953.

The 1950-53 model lineup didn't change much from the '48/'49 offerings either. The 62 series, which accounted for most Cadillac sales, comprised a four-door sedan, two-door sedanet, Coupe de Ville hardtop, and two-door convertible. The 60 Special remained a long-wheelbase four-door sedan only; the Series 75 offered a limousine and a sedan on a 147-inch wheelbase. The 61 sedans and sedanets sold for about $350 less than the equivalent 62s, but they vanished after 1951. Cadillac saw no further purpose in retaining these lower-priced models, and in 1952 began concentrating exclusively on the uppermost end of the market.

The most notable arrival for 1953 was the ultra-luxurious, limited-production Eldorado convertible. Only 532 were built, tagged at $7750 each, which made this the most expensive American production car that year. It predicted things to come from GM's volume models in 1954 with its cut-down panoramic (wraparound) windshield. The Eldorado also featured a metal boot that completely hid the convertible top when lowered. Hydra-Matic had been standard on all Cadillacs since 1952, but some models were sold with Dynaflow Drive in 1953. A fire at the Hydra-Matic plant in Willow Run, Michigan forced Cadillac to use a few Buick transmissions that year just to keep production going.

Model year 1954 witnessed major styling overhauls at Olds and Buick and also saw a new line of longer, lower, wider, and more powerful Cadillacs. Wheelbases were 129 inches for the 62 series, 133 for the 60 Special, and 147 for the

1953 Series 62 Coupe deVille

1953 Fleetwood Series 75 Imperial sedan

1954 Series 62 Coupe deVille

1954 Fleetwood Series 60 Special sedan

1954 Fleetwood Series 75 limousine

Series 75. The 331-cid engine got a boost in horsepower to 230. Cadillac now decided to make money with the Eldorado, rather than continue it as an unprofitable "image" car. Accordingly, it was given a much less unique, production-derived body mounted on the 62 chassis, and a reduced price of $5738. These measures resulted in 2150 unit sales, which doubled in 1955. For 1956, the Eldorado line comprised the Seville coupe and Biarritz convertible, each priced at $6556. Incidentally, this was the first use of the Seville name by Cadillac, although it was also picked up by DeSoto for its four-door hardtop that year.

The Eldorado regained its own distinctive styling touches for 1955; the most noticeable were its rear fenders, reshaped into sharply pointed fins with small, round taillights mounted below. This was carried over on the '56 models. Other Cadillacs continued with the smaller kicked-up tailfin/taillight, which by now had become a styling

hallmark. Division sales, which topped 100,000 for the first time in 1950, continued to improve through the middle years of the decade. In 1955, Cadillac sold over 150,000 units, the highest number ever in any calendar year. Even this was only a temporary plateau, as production would break 200,000 in the 1960s, and reach a high of 266,000 in 1969.

The disappearance of the low-priced Series 61 in 1952 had an indirect bearing on Cadillac's sales dominance in the years that followed. From now on, Cadillac would again produce luxury models only. Packard, on the other hand, was still marketing a line of middle-priced cars, called 200s through 1952 and Clippers from 1953. These represented the bulk of Packard production in those years and cost the firm its time-honored cachét of exclusivity. Such an approach was anathema to Cadillac Division: The luxury market was strong, so why even consider a cheaper

1955 Series 62 Coupe deVille

1955 Eldorado convertible

55

model? Packard, of course, was a struggling independent, and felt it needed the extra sales volume its 200/Clipper models promised. But Cadillac's policy was vindicated in the sales charts. Throughout the '50s, it handily outsold Packard, even counting sales of the latter's cheaper models.

Packard trailed Cadillac in styling and engineering, if not sales, as early as 1948. Its restyle that year was clumsy and bloated. The firm's 356-cid L-head straight eight was smooth and powerful, but it was also very heavy. Limited by its aging design, this engine simply wouldn't be able to stay with Cadillac in the horsepower race. In its last year, 1954, the Packard straight eight had been coaxed into delivering up to 212 bhp; Cadillac's V-8 that same year had an output of 230 bhp, which would go up to 270 in 1955.

Lincoln wasn't much of a threat to Cadillac in those years, either. Lincoln retained its prewar styling and an unreliable, underpowered V-12

engine for its 1948 models. For 1949, there was new styling and a flathead V-8, neither of which was as pleasing as Cadillac's aircraft-inspired lines and overhead-valve V-8. Lincoln didn't get a modern short-stroke ohv V-8 until 1952; Packard's didn't arrive until 1955. Cadillac had only to refine and update its V-8 each year to stay easily ahead of the competition.

Packard's luxury models disappeared after 1956 (and the marque itself after 1958), though another challenge was mounted by Chrysler with its revitalized 1957 Imperial. In 1961, Lincoln took another crack at Cadillac with its new, well-built, and nicely styled Continental sedan and unique four-door convertible. But neither Lincoln nor Imperial ever built more than 40,000 cars a year, and often their output was quite a bit less. The luxury field in the 1950s was completely dominated by Cadillac. The same was true in the '60s and the '70s. Beyond a shadow of a doubt, it will be true of the '80s as well.

1955 Fleetwood Series 75 eight-passenger sedan

1956 Fleetwood Series 75 limousine

1956 Eldorado Biarritz convertible

1956 Eldorado Seville hardtop coupe

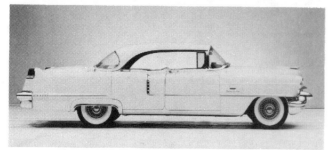

1956 Series 62 Sedan deVille

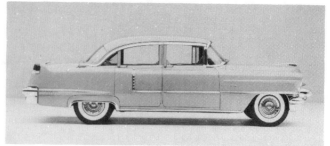

1956 Series 62 sedan

SPOTLIGHT: Birth of the Tailfin: 1948-49

Many critical students of postwar automotive design say Cadillac styling was never better than in 1948-49. The division fielded its first all-new car since the war in '48. The following year, Cadillac left styling well enough alone, but debuted one of the industry's first true hardtops. For the first time, the rear of a car had definition and interest. The tailfin did more to establish Cadillac's identity in the late '40s and into the '50s than any other single design element.

Patterned after the wartime Lockheed P-38 aircraft, the '48-'49 fin was beautifully integrated with the contours of the rear fenders which, for the time being, were separate, bolt-on units. While rear fenders protruded from the bodysides, the front fenders flowed smoothly into the doors. The overall shape was sweeping and streamlined, accented perfectly by the rear-end treatment.

The Cadillac Series 61 and 62 were almost identical in external appearance in these two years. The easiest way to tell them apart is by their front fenders: The 62 has a bright metal splash guard there, while the 61 doesn't. The 62 can also be distinguished by small, horizontal chrome bars on its rear fenders. The long-wheelbase 60 Special, which wears its new styling equally well, is devoid of side trim except for a

1948 Series 62 "sedanet" five-passenger coupe

1948 60 Special five-passenger touring sedan

1949 Series 62 Coupe deVille

delicate "dummy" scoop at the leading edge of the rear fender. The 1949 Coupe de Ville "hardtop-convertible" was a brand-new style, one of the first hardtops in volume production. But the fastback coupe or sedanet is still the best-looking model, at least in the eyes of many discerning students of style.

"The Envious Cry Out That It Cannot Be Done" Showcars and Experiments

1958 automatic-top Biarritz convertible

From his very first GM design, the 1927 La-Salle, Harley Earl's efforts had been highly regarded by engineers. But the public taste was always paramount in Earl's mind. The postwar "dream cars" built for testing and exhibiting new design ideas were created mainly to gauge the *public's* reaction to a line, a contour, a detail. The usual venues for such displays were the fabulous GM Motoramas, those memorable extravaganzas of glamor, glitter, and gladiolas, held sporadically between 1949 and 1961. "A Motorama is more than a good show and good promotion," Harley Earl said. "Frankly it makes my styling job easier, as visitors express themselves vividly, and by the time hundreds of thousands of these critics have examined your show and commented on your exhibits you have a firm idea of their likes and dislikes." Eventually, GM discontinued the Motoramas, because their publicity value didn't make up for the fact that they gave the competition a sneak preview of forthcoming GM designs. But while they lasted, the Motoramas were blessed by a stellar variety of experimental Cadillacs.

The flush-fitting convertible top cover seen on the first Eldorado had actually been sketched by the Art & Colour Studio some years before the car was shown in 1953. For the 1952 Motorama, Cadillac tried the same idea on a special Series 62 convertible. This car had custom upholstery and dual rear antennas, but was otherwise stock. It received favorable comment, so Earl ordered the top cover into production for the limited-edition '53 Eldorado.

Though the Eldorado was ostensibly a production car, the fact that relatively few were made in its first year suggests it was really more a method of testing ideas than a serious sales effort. Its deep-angle panoramic windshield, disappearing top, boldly downswept beltline, chrome wire wheels, and leather interior were items that all

found their way into various mass-market GM cars in succeeding years. The Eldorado's real purpose was to keep Cadillac as much a styling leader in the mid '50s as it had been in 1948—at least in the public mind. It was a low, lean car with a minimum of brightwork, and it drew crowds like a Yankees-Dodgers game. To this extent, the '53 Eldorado was a considerable success.

At the same time the Eldorado premiered, Cadillac also showed two one-of-a-kind creations which anticipated styling ideas farther down the road—the Orleans and Le Mans. The latter was a short (115-inch wheelbase) fiberglass two-seater. Its front end predicted fairly accurately the styling of the 1954-55 production models, though the massive front looked a bit out of proportion on the short body. Unlike many show machines, this car actually ran—and rapidly—thanks to a 250-bhp derivation of the production 331-cid V-8. Its steering was quick and positive. Its roadholding wasn't bad, though *Motor Trend* magazine found it "definitely too heavy and spongy for competition." Competition, of course, was the last thing Cadillac had in mind. The Le Mans accomplished two things: it previewed the forthcoming production frontal styling, and it promoted the feasibility of fiberglass body construction. The car's front end duly appeared on all Cadillacs a year later and, of course, fiberglass was successfully adopted for the contemporary 1953 Corvette.

But the Orleans was more interesting to Cadillac watchers than Le Mans, because the kind of people who bought Cadillacs could relate better to luxury six-seaters. The Orleans was certainly that, and more besides: It was GM's first four-door hardtop.

Harley Earl had ordered the two-door hardtop body style into production for 1949 partly based on the opinion of one staffman's wife. "She always wanted convertibles, but didn't put the top down," Earl said. "She just thought they were better looking. Her husband promptly pitched in with some of the rest of us who were chasing a similar idea, and for 1949 we had the hardtop . . . We were pretty sure this was a basically good idea, but we were certain of it when we set up a display of all cars for a bankers' convention and asked these reputedly conservative men to select cars they would like to own. Sixty percent of them picked hardtops." The Orleans was simply a follow-up to the Coupe deVille idea and expanded the hardtop's appeal to people who liked its lines, but insisted on four doors.

Earl got the idea for a four-door hardtop during a visit to Italy, where he saw a contemporary production Lancia sedan designed with no center "B" pillars. The Orleans proved the idea was workable from an engineering standpoint and

would be a smash with customers. It was a preview of things to come: Four-door hardtops appeared for 1955 in the Buick and Oldsmobile lines and in 1956, Cadillac offered this body style as the Sedan deVille. By then, the rest of the industry was scurrying to catch up. This is another example of GM's willingness to risk millions on what would turn out to be a successful design theme. It's one of the reasons GM is so large and profitable today.

The greatest number of Cadillac dream cars in a single year shared the spotlight in 1954. Three specials were displayed: the Park Avenue, La Espada, and El Camino. La Espada and El Camino were basically the same car, one with a top and one topless. Like Le Mans, they had short wheelbases but massive, Cadillac-style front

1952 Motorama showcar featured metal top cover.

President and Mrs. Eisenhower try out 1953 Eldorado.

Orleans four-door hardtop debuted at '53 Motorama.

Despite name, Le Mans of '53 was no sports car.

El Camino was featured at '54 Motorama.

Sporty La Espada shared spotlight with El Camino in '54.

Park Avenue inspired production Eldorado Brougham.

Eldorado Brougham showcar was built for '55 Motorama.

Brougham town car for '56 had fiberglass body.

Cyclone of '59 featured rocketship styling, on-board radar.

ends. Their tailfin shape predicted the design used on the 1955 Eldorado and the 1958 standard line; their front-end appearance was picked up in modified form for the 1957 models; their quad headlamps predicted a feature of the Eldorado Brougham; and the El Camino's roofline was echoed in '57 too. The El Camino name, of course, appeared in 1959 on a sporty Chevrolet pick-up

based on that division's passenger-car body and styling.

Road & Track magazine, which had called Le Mans "that thing," considered La Espada and El Camino "beautifully done." Both featured contrasting aluminum side trim accentuating a "cove" area behind the front wheel openings. This idea found its way onto the restyled 1956 Corvette. Like Le Mans, La Espada and El Camino were not intended for production; besides, they were too small for the typical Cadillac buyer. Again, the show crowd was drawn more to the Park Avenue, which was very much in the running for production: In fact, it was the forebear of the fabulous Eldorado Brougham.

The Park Avenue was a clean four-door "town sedan" of elegant, though substantial, proportions, yet somewhat smaller overall than the '54 production models. Though it retained center pillars, its window frames were very thin and neatly followed the contour of the roof, which was covered in brushed stainless steel (one of Harley Earl's favorite design touches). The tailfins were modest affairs, each carrying three vertically stacked bullet-shaped taillamps. The Park Avenue was a tremendous hit. The 1954 Motorama had not even closed when Earl approached division general manager Don Ahrens with a proposal to build another show car for 1955, and a production version for 1956. Ahrens agreed, and the Brougham project was officially underway.

Cadillac Engineering was now brought into the picture, and delivered the prototype chassis only 74 days before the 1955 Motorama was scheduled to open. Last minute preparations were hectic. Just before press night, as Earl was breathing a sigh of relief, the Brougham showcar fell off its jacks, smashing a fender and a bumper. Chaos reigned as Cadillac workers scurried like beavers to repair the damage. But the next day, when 5000 advance show goers arrived, there was the light-green car revolving quietly and sedately on its turntable. If Harley Earl had had any sense of history that day, he would have muttered a quote to himself from "The Penalty of Leadership": "The envious cry out that it cannot be done."

Earl personally helped evaluate public reaction to the Eldorado Brougham, and it was highly enthusiastic. Thousands of brochures were handed to admirers. The Brougham, they read, "was created with the intent of capturing the appeal of those who demand the finest product . . . a compact, personalized automobile, easy to operate and employing our latest knowledge of styling and engineering. Only 54 inches in height and 210 inches in length, it features low, sweeping lines . . . graceful contours of roof and hood, a unique pillarless door design . . . and great areas of vision. Among its interior innovations are specially designed lounge seats, a distinctive vanity case and a unique instrument panel. Its performance is highlighted by a special high-powered Cadillac engine." The 1955 Brougham followed the La Espada/El Camino lead with dual headlights, though some time passed before every state allowed this arrangement. (For this reason, the production model was actually illegal in several states for a short time after its introduction, though this was quickly corrected by legislative action. It may have been the last time a law was passed to accommodate a car manufacturer.)

Cadillac promised Brougham production would begin on a limited basis in 1956, but it didn't make the deadline. The cars were not fully tested until December of that year. To fill the gap, a pre-production prototype was exhibited, along with a custom-built derivative, the Brougham Town Car. The Town Car had a fiberglass body and was slightly longer than the sedan. Apparently, this design caused little interest, for only one example was produced. A better reception might have led to the rebirth of a classic body style.

The production 1957 Eldorado Brougham was the ultimate in Harley Earl's long line of experimental Cadillacs designed to test ideas, the best of which were put into production. But though it was good looking and utterly unique, it was unsuccessful in the marketplace. After 400 examples were built for 1957 and 304 in 1958, production was transferred to Pininfarina. The Italians built 99 more for 1959 and 101 for 1960 before the Brougham faded from the scene.

The next Cadillac dream car to appear in the '50s was really just a minor modification to a production model: the special 1958 Biarritz convertible, of which only five were built. This car's principal attraction was that it "eliminated all manual effort in raising, lowering and securing a convertible top at the touch of a button." A humidity control automatically raised the top and windows when it sensed rain—whether or not the driver was nearby. When down, the top was covered by a flush-fitting steel panel like that of the 1953 Eldorado. The top mechanism operated through four electric motors.

The automatic-top Biarritz made no impression on the public. Like Ford's retractable "Skyliner" hardtop-convertible, it was seen as mechanical overkill, even in those days when the public's fascination with gadgetry was high. Cadillac owners, apparently, were quite capable of remembering to raise the top and windows when it rained, thank you.

The Cadillac Cyclone was Harley Earl's last dream car, displayed in 1959 just after the founder of GM styling had retired. A steel-bodied two-seater on a 104-inch wheelbase, the Cyclone was the shortest car to bear the Cadillac name in 50 years. Styling was of the "rocket ship" school, with a pointed snoot, bubble top, cockpit interior, and sliding doors—all of which were no doubt inspired by TV space operas of the day. The clear plastic canopy swung up when a door was slid back, but the Cyclone was hard to enter gracefully because of its dogleg windshield. Powered by a standard 325-bhp Cadillac V-8 engine with low-profile carb, cross-flow aluminum radiator, and twin cooling fans, the Cyclone was lightning-fast when it toured the oval at the new Daytona International Speedway, where the car was introduced on the track's opening day.

Cadillac insisted the Cyclone was strictly an experiment, and indeed, some of its features were pretty far out. The muffler and exhaust system, for example, were carried *inside* the engine compartment; the exhaust was ducted out ahead of the front wheels. There was also a "proximity warning device," a kind of on-board radar system. Two 10-inch aluminum reflectors were mounted behind the car's twin front "nose cones," with a transmitter and receiver built into the front fenders. The transmitter sent out waves and the reflectors picked them up again as they bounced back from an object lying dead ahead. The driver was warned of an object's presence by a flashing light or warning buzzer. As the distance between car and obstacle decreased, the light would flash faster and the buzzer got louder. The system was rumoured to be in the works as an option for 1960 or '61, but it never materialized, probably because the distraction caused by the warning signals were a terrific annoyance, especially when making a turn in traffic. (A cruder version of automotive radar was also tried by Packard in 1956. This one actually locked up all four brakes if any object came into range, which proved to be most embarrassing on crowded city streets.)

Although Bill Mitchell was named director of GM Styling in May, 1954, Harley Earl stayed on as vice-president until his retirement in November, 1958. Most of the Earl show cars were chopped up or modified after he left, though some have survived in GM's dusty warehouses. Mitchell, of course, designed many show car exotics of his own, but they tended to be sporty vehicles of the Corvette/Corvair type or mild derivations of production models like the Riviera or Toronado. Cadillac's days as a progenitor of idea cars were over, ending with the Motorama itself in 1961. But many features predicted by the Cadillac show-cars eventually did go into production models.

Harley Earl always maintained the validity of his exercises. "They are not altogether Buck Rogers vehicles ... They are small opinion laboratories ... some experimental features have been so promptly approved by Motorama visitors that they have immediately been incorporated into production models. It is equally true that we have built into many of the dream cars some downright impractical things, or at any rate, features that appear to be impractical today. You can never tell about tomorrow."

The fins of change: 1949 (left) and 1959 (right)

"That Which Is Good or Great Makes Itself Known" 1957-1966

Cadillac had a watershed year in 1957 with many engineering changes and a new bodyshell. The most important technical innovation was a new frame with a tubular center X-member that gave increased rigidity. Because the body could sit lower on the chassis than before, the floor of the '57 car was dropped three inches closer to the ground compared to its 1956 counterpart. Horsepower of standard models rose to 300 bhp while Eldorados got an optional 325-bhp engine with two four-barrel carburetors. Refinements were made to the power steering, power brakes, and Hydra-Matic transmission. The '57 model was a lively performer despite its considerable size and weight. Fuel consumption was also surprisingly moderate.

The new body styling featured a wide, flat hood; a lower, wider egg-crate grille; and prominent gullwing front bumpers with pointed rubber-tipped "Dagmar" bumper guards. At the back, standard models inherited squared-off fins like those on the '56 Eldorado, though they were slightly lower and longer and were canted forward slightly. There were new, small round taillights mounted at the base of the fins and above the exhaust outlets in the rear bumper.

For the first time, the 60 Special appeared in pillarless four-door hardtop form instead of sedan style. But the sportiest Cadillacs continued to be the two Eldorados, the Seville hardtop coupe (continued from 1956), and the Biarritz convertible. Each carried the same $7286 price tag. These models continued to use the popular, cast "sabre-spoke" wheels introduced in 1955. Eldorado front-end styling was little different from the standard models, but the rear fender and trunk lid treatment was entirely individual. The bumpers were highly polished sand-cast aluminum, and wrapped around to the rear wheel openings. The

rear deck curved down sharply to a rounded lower panel which contained a frenched-in license plate housing between the half bumpers. The rear fenders were capped by prominent, pointy, chrome-edged fins set just slightly inboard of the

1957 Series 75 Limousine

1957 Series 62 Coupe deVille

1957 60 Special four-door hardtop

rear fender sides. Most optional equipment on the standard line was offered at no cost on the Eldorado, with the exception of tinted glass and air conditioning.

Most spectacular by far was the 1957 Eldorado Brougham. At $13,074 a copy, this four-door hardtop was GM's direct reply to Ford Motor Company's Continental Mark II, which appeared the previous year. Eldorado is Spanish for "the gilded one," an appropriate "first name" for the lush, luxurious Brougham. It had more tinsel and chrome than any other car in America—it was the automotive equivalent of Las Vegas. The carpet was nylon or lambskin at the buyer's discretion. The Brougham's sheetmetal was not shared with any other Cadillac, and its four headlights were also unique to this one model. Its roof, covered by brushed stainless steel, stood only 55.5 inches from the ground. Suspension was by rubber "air bags" pressurized by a small compressor (powered by its own electric motor) and regulated by leveling valves. Narrow, one-inch whitewalls were an industry styling first. The Brougham had "power everything": windows, seats, steering, brakes. Among its standard ammenities were a personalized notepad and pencil, a tissue dispenser, and a glovebox vanity with six silver

magnetized tumblers and a perfume dispenser loaded with Arpége. Cadillac had literally made its Motorama show car a reality which could be ordered at the down-home dealership. All it took was $13,074.

The 1958 Cadillac continued with design themes typical of the late '50s: short hood, long rear deck, and mounds of chrome, all on a "longer-lower-wider" body. Quad headlamps now were legal in all states and these were featured on standard models as well as the Brougham. The "Dagmar" bumper guards were moved farther out and shrank in size, the grille was wider and more sparkling. The fins were canted outward slightly. Air suspension would be all the rage for a brief couple of years and was available as an extra-cost item in '58. Chrome speed streaks decorated the rear quarter panels of all standard models. The 60 Special featured fender skirts and continued to use a textured aluminum applique on the lower halves of the rear fenders and part of the rear doors. Interiors were as luxurious as the exotic names of their upholstery materials: Moroccan cloth, Tunisian cloth, and something called "Elascofab." There were two engines: the standard 310-bhp V-8 or the optional 335-bhp version with triple two-barrel carburetors. The 335 was

1957 Eldorado Biarritz convertible

1958 Series 62 Sedan deVille

1957 Eldorado Seville hardtop coupe

1958 Eldorado Seville hardtop coupe

1957 Eldorado Brougham

1958 60 Special four-door hardtop

standard on Eldorados. Though the '58 looked vastly different from the '57, it still used the same X-member frame.

The summit of garishness was reached literally with the towering tailfins of the restyled 1959 line. These were the highest fins in the industry, and had twin bullet-shaped taillights for that authentic rocket-ship look. While nobody probably bothered to measure these fins, they were no doubt taller than those of Virgil Exner's Chrysler products. They looked ridiculous, and were condemned as excessive even at the time. At the end of the '50s, the public was beginning to tire of fins, though they'd still be around for a few more years.

The radical styling of the '59 model tended to obscure its completely new body. The huge compound-curve windshield wrapped up slightly into the roof, and wheelbase was increased to 130 inches. The redesigned grille was divided by a thick, horizontal chrome bar and was studded with lots of little bullets, as on the '58 models. A similar "grille" (actually an applique) ran across the lower back panel above the rear bumper. All four-door sedans in '59 were actually hardtops; none had the stationary "B" post. Cadillac attempted to satisfy everyone's styling tastes by offering them with a choice of two different rooflines, a six-window style and a four-window. The former had rear quarter windows and a huge backlight that curved upward into the gently sloping roof; the latter had no rear quarter windows, a

huge wraparound rear window, and a flat roofline that extended slightly beyond the backlight. The 60 Special again used its own distinctive side and rear fender trim, though all body styles now featured fender skirts. Horsepower was still on the rise in 1959: up to 325 bhp in standard models or 345 bhp with triple carbs for the Eldorado. Saginaw rotary-valve power steering was standard across-the-board. Eldorados switched from the "sabre-spoke" wheels to stamped steel wheels like lesser models.

For 1959-60, production of the redesigned Eldorado Brougham was transferred from the U.S. to Pininfarina of Italy where the cars were built by hand. It was cheaper to do it this way because none of the Brougham's sheetmetal, glass, or trim interchanged with the regular line. The Broughams did share mechanical components, floors, dashes, wheels, bumpers, skirts, and headlamp shells with Fleetwood models, but they were shorter and narrower overall. Unhappily, the Italian Broughams lacked the assembly quality of the 1957-58 Detroit versions. Large amounts of lead had to be used to fill low spots in the bodies, so the paint surface often cracked. The cars still used the trouble-prone air suspension and cost as much as they had in 1958, though fewer were built (only 99 in 1959 and 101 in 1960). After 1960, the Eldorado Brougham was put to rest—one of the few Cadillac models in the '50s that was not profitable for the division.

Styling for 1960 was a toned-down facelift of

1959 Eldorado Biarritz convertible

1959 Fleetwood Series 75 limousine

1959 Series 62 Coupe deVille

1959 Series 62 six-window Sedan deVille

1959 Eldorado Brougham by Pininfarina

1960 Eldorado Brougham by Pininfarina

the '59 look. The bullet taillights disappeared in favor of thin red lenses at the trailing edges of the fins, which were much lower and more restrained than before. All '60 models used less chrome, though the grillework was still busy, with lots of little shiny bullets arrayed in a cross-hatch pattern. Front fender ornaments were functional: They doubled as housings for turn signal indicator lights. The 60 Special gained a fabric roof cover keyed to body color and shed its shiny side trim. The Eldorado Seville hardtop made its last appearance. (You could tell a '59 or '60 Eldorado from other Cadillacs by the Eldorado name in block letters on the front fenders and by this model's generally more garish trim.) Accessories continued to proliferate with such items as cruise control, air conditioning, power door locks, fog lamps, and air suspension.

Slumping sales in the late '50s had led to an industry-wide turnaround in styling and overall size. Cadillac changed accordingly for '61 with a slightly smaller but neater and more sculptured design. The fins were still present but were even lower than in 1960. There were also curious lower fins which flared outward from the base of the rear fenders. The grille, still recognizeably Cadillac, was now convex instead of flat and incorporated the headlights at its outer ends. It continued to use lots of tiny bullets. The hood and front fenders were now the same height and formed a full-width flat surface. But 1961 was a year of reconsideration by many car buyers, including those in the luxury market. While Cadillac's huge production lead over its rivals was not seriously affected, total output for '61 was down by about 4000 units.

The division had taken a fresh look at the Eldorado series, and decided to offer it only as a convertible beginning in 1961 through the last of the rear-drive models in 1966. In these years, Eldorados were mainly trim variations of the standard Series 62 convertible. In the 62 line itself, a new body style was offered. This was a short-deck pillarless sedan, a twin to the regular four- and six-window four-doors, except for its seven-inch shorter overall length, which gave it a rather odd appearance. Prices in 1961 ranged from a low of $5080 for the 62 sedan to $6477 for the Eldorado Biarritz convertible; the Fleetwood 75 limousine led the line at $9748. Air conditioning was $474 to $624 extra, depending on model. Steering was improved for better maneuverability and refinements were made to the suspension and braking systems.

The 1962 Cadillac retained the same bodyshell and general lines as the '61 car. (In the late '50s and early '60s, Cadillac and the rest of GM observed two-year styling cycles.) One throwback to earlier years was the 1962's pseudo rear "grille," an item which had been eliminated in 1961. The facelifted grille was flatter and combination park-

ing/fog lights appeared in the bumper tips below the dual headlights. Cornering lights were offered in Cadillac's options repertoire for the first time. These were mounted in the forward part of the front fenders and shined whenever the turn signals were used so as to light up the corner areas to the front and sides of the car. A new safety measure was the dual-circuit brake system with separate pistons, hydraulic lines, and fluid reservoirs for front and rear brakes. This assured that should one brake line fail the driver would still be able to stop the car. Later, this feature was mandated by the federal government for all cars sold in the U.S.

The short-deck Series 62 sedan was given its own name, "Town Sedan," which distinguished it from the standard-length 62 sedan. Another short-deck model appeared in 1962's new DeVille series, christened the "Park Avenue." This was the first year that Cadillac really began to distinguish between the 62 and the DeVille in luxury and price. A 62 coupe, for example, cost $5025 while its DeVille counterpart listed at $5385.

Following its two-year styling cycle, Cadillac completely redesigned its 1963 line and made important mechanical changes. There was a brand-new roofline that was particularly noticeable on coupes. Designers had lengthened the rear deck by seven inches simply by shortening the greenhouse, though no passenger room was sacrificed. Overall, the cars had a look of greater size with a clearly defined hood and longer, restyled front

1960 Fleetwood Series 60 Special

1960 Eldorado Biarritz convertible

1962 Series 62 six-window Sedan deVille

1963 four-window Sedan deVille

1964 Series 62 coupe

1964 Fleetwood Series 75 limousine

1964 Fleetwood 60 Special sedan

1964 Fleetwood Eldorado Biarritz convertible

fenders. The "double-deck" grille treatment was reminiscent of '59 styling but was very much more subdued. At the upper end of the price spectrum, the 60 Special offered an optional all-leather interior and a padded vinyl top which was also available for the Coupe de Ville. The tailfins had a

still lower profile, and would soon disappear entirely. All Cadillacs except the 75 had new windshields. Options available for the first time in '63 included a tilt-adjustable steering wheel, AM-FM radio, and a combined air conditioning/heater control panel. A newly designed V-8 engine appeared which was shorter and narrower than the previous powerplant.

In 1964, we were reminded that the Cadillac V-8—the engine on which the company had built its fortunes—was then half a century old. That which was good or great, as Theodore MacManus said many years before, had certainly made itself known. The year was marked by an elegant model line which is considered by many students of the marque to be a high point for Cadillac design and engineering.

That year's Eldorado was the only model without fender skirts and wore its Biarritz designation for the last time. The open rear wheel wells gave it a sporty touch. Basic styling on all models was changed little from 1963. The most noticeable differences were redesigned bumper ends and taillight housings. Besides the Eldorado, 10 other body styles were offered in '64; five were available with a padded vinyl top, the latest thing for fashion-conscious customers. In line with the general trend toward larger overall size, Cadillac dropped the slow-selling short-deck sedans. The instrument panel was restyled and front seat belts became standard equipment on all models. The engine was bored and stroked to 429 cubic inches and now developed 340 horsepower. A larger exhaust system was added to meet the performance requirements of the larger engine. The most popular of several newly introduced creature comforts was Cadillac's automatic climate control, which maintained a desired temperature regardless of conditions, all with one dial. Another new feature was "Twilight Sentinel" which automatically turned the headlights on and off as needed. A built-in delay timer kept the lights on for a few minutes after the ignition was switched off so passengers could see their way to the door. This was a neat and unique item that is still offered on current Cadillacs.

The 1965 model was all new: Everything changed except the engine. Styling was completely transformed with strong geometric shapes and wide, flat body panels. A wide egg-crate grille was strongly reminiscent of the great 1941 models. Headlights were vertically stacked and tailfins disappeared for good. Cornering lights were now integral with the front bumpers, and vinyl roofs were available on six models. The Eldorado convertible regained its fender skirts. Interiors of all models were also fully redesigned. The Series 62 was renamed Calais, though the DeVille series was now the best-seller. Calais sales would decline until the name was dropped in 1977. The Series 75 retained its 1964 bodyshell and styling for the same reason that it had held onto its prewar looks through 1949: Sales of the 75 were very low, and Cadillac saw no reason to update the model every time the rest of the line got a major style change. The 60 Special reverted to its old 133-inch wheelbase for a considerable increase in rear passenger room. When fitted with a padded vinyl roof, the 60 Special became the Fleetwood Brougham. It was Cadillac's most luxurious owner-driven sedan.

An important structural innovation for '65 was a completely new "perimeter-type" chassis. This featured frame rails designed to run along and under the full perimeter of the bodyshell. This completely reversed previous design principles but it resulted in better overall balance because the engine could be moved forward six inches without disturbing weight distribution. The new design also provided a lower floor tunnel. To match the new chassis a revised rear axle housing and rear suspension were developed. Drivetrain revisions included standard Turbo Hydra-Matic transmission for all models and an automatic lock-in device for the cruise control. New options were a telescoping steering column adjustment, an automatic leveling device (standard on 60 Special and Eldorado), and a new power door lock system.

In 1966, Cadillac ran true to form with only a mild facelift. There was less chrome and more conservative ornamentation. It was now time for the 75 to catch up with the standard line in styling and these new long-wheelbase cars were pleasing to the eye. In all, Cadillac offered a dozen models. Due to its popularity, the Fleetwood Brougham became a model in its own right at the top of the regular lineup. On the Brougham's comprehensive list of no-cost luxury extras were fold-down rear seat writing tables, rear foot hassocks, and a full-leather interior.

As mentioned, 1966 was the last year for the rear-drive Eldorado, and there would not be another Eldorado convertible model until 1971. The '66 version featured "soft-ray" tinted glass all around, even for the rear window in the convertible top. Genuine walnut was used on the upper door panels and window sills of the Eldorado, as well as in the 60 Special and Fleetwood Brougham. All '66 Cadillacs had a new variable-ratio power steering gear.

Its preeminence in the luxury field, won through long years of growth and innovation, had stood Cadillac in good sted during the late '50s and early '60s. In these years the division simply rolled over its competition, finishing 9th, 10th or 11th in the annual production race, often out-producing Chrysler as well as Lincoln and Imperial. Production ranged around 150,000 cars a year, an incredible total in the luxury-price field. And in those twin banner years of 1965 and 1966, Cadillac averaged about 200,000 cars each twelve months, setting

1965 Fleetwood Eldorado convertible

1965 Calais coupe

1966 Fleetwood Brougham sedan

1966 Fleetwood Series 75 limousine

1966 Coupe deVille

its own all-time record. With the exception of 1970, the division has never been under 200,000 cars a year since. Often, production has exceeded 300,000 units. But despite this success, there were still greater achievements to come in 1967 and beyond.

SPOTLIGHT:
The Eldorado Brougham

In an attempt to one-up its rival in Dearborn, Cadillac fielded the ultra-luxurious Eldorado Brougham in 1957 as a direct reply to the Continental Mark II. The Mark II was priced at $10,000, but Cadillac listed the exotic Brougham at $13,074—a definite note of price defiance. But both companies lost money on these super-cars. The Mark II was dropped in 1958 in favor of the "Mark III," which was cheaper to build and offered a wider range of body styles.

Cadillac farmed out Brougham production to Pininfarina in Italy for 1959-60 before dropping the model, but the Italian cars were not nearly as well made as the 1957-58 Detroit-built versions.

This Eldorado Brougham

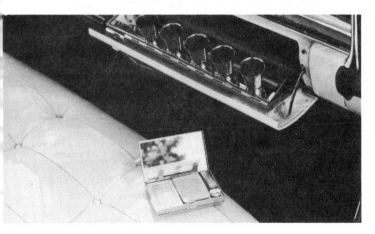

is a 1958 edition. It rides a 126-inch wheelbase, several inches shorter than the year's standard Series 62. It bears many styling touches beloved by Harley Earl, including a brushed stainless-steel roof, hooded "quad" headlights, and an egg-crate grille dominated by bold, pointed, gullwing bumper guards. Detail touches are the ornate spoke-style wheel covers, thin-section taillights built neatly into the lower portion of the tailfins, and fake air vents atop the front fenders, one of which surrounds the radio antenna. Inside, this example contains the full set of six magnetized drinking cups and the original make-up kit.

Car owned by Mr. & Mrs. Dale Woods. Photographs by Bud Juneau.

"If the Leader Truly Leads, He Remains— The Leader" 1967-74

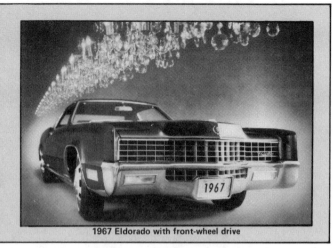
1967 Eldorado with front-wheel drive

In the '50s, Cadillac built the tailfin bandwagon which the rest of the industry eagerly jumped on. Yet in the '60s, Cadillac led the field away from gimmicky, flamboyant styling. This apparent contradiction is nothing more than an example of shrewd market judgment: Cadillac continued to dominate the luxury field as the '60s

1967 Eldorado prototype under construction

Clay model XP-727 no. 2, photographed in June, 1961

1967 Fleetwood Eldorado

faded into the '70s. If there is any doubt about Cadillac's astuteness, consider the magnificent front-wheel-drive Eldorado.

The 1967 Eldorado was an all-new car, one of the few that deserve that label. Mechanically, it was derived from the Oldsmobile Toronado but its styling was quite different. It was created, of course, by Bill Mitchell's GM Styling Staff which had been working with the five-seat "personal car" theme since 1961. The Mitchell group's first major accomplishment in this area was the 1963 Buick Riviera. The Eldorado had its origins in the Riviera-like XP-727 clay model, which went through three revisions before finally being discarded as "too contemporary." Its successor was XP-784, the first design planned around front-wheel-drive. The direct antecedant to the 1967 Eldorado was XP-820, which with minor revisions became XP-825. It was this study which was presented to management in May, 1964. It was one of the great shapes of the '60s, completely lacking in rough spots, perfect from every angle. Yet, it was sufficiently formal-looking to be consistent with Cadillac styling tradition. (For awhile, management considered calling its new car "La Salle" but because of its history as Cadillac's only failure, the name was ruled out.)

In addition to superb styling, the '67 Eldorado was blessed with equally fine engineering. What the division wanted was a large, luxurious car with all its traditional virtues allied to outstanding roadability. To achieve this, Cadillac used its 429 cubic-inch, 340-horsepower V-8 teamed with a "split" transmission: The torque converter and gearbox were separate from each other, linked by a chain drive and sprocket. The key to this arrangement was the chain, a development of GM's Hydra-Matic Division and Borg-Warner. It was unbreakable, yet flexible, light, and not too costly. The split transmission made the engine-drivetrain package quite compact.

Front-wheel drive gave the Eldorado almost neutral handling characteristics. *Automobile*

Quarterly editor Don Vorderman, who gave the car his magazine's third Design and Engineering Award in six years, noted that in cornering, the Eldorado developed "a mounting understeer when under full power, but this is easily neutralized by backing off the accelerator, at which time the tail will move but in the classic FWD tradition . . . It is doubtful that one owner in a thousand will drive the car this way, but it does speak volumes on how thoroughly Cadillac engineers have done their job."

The Eldorado was not greatly changed until 1971, when it acquired a heavier, bulkier body and a companion convertible model. It continued in this form through 1974, with inflation and government-mandated safety and emissions equipment escalating its price each year. From around $6500 in 1957, the price of an Eldorado had risen to nearly $10,000 in 1974. The first-generation front-drive Eldorados (1967-70) are highly prized by collectors, and their value has been on the upswing for several years now. For all their luxury and size, those cars were remarkable road machines—more capable on a bit of twisty blacktop than many so-called sports cars. Anyone who thinks that big American cars don't handle well hasn't driven an early front-drive Eldorado.

Though the Eldorado accounted for upwards of 20,000 annual sales through 1971, and 40,000 or 50,000 thereafter, the big Cadillac sedans and coupes continued to dominate production in the late '60s and early '70s. Through 1976, the standard line consisted of three series: the low-priced Calais coupe and sedans; the top-selling DeVille hardtop coupe, hardtop sedan, sedan, and convertible; and the Fleetwood line, which included the 60 Special, 60 Special Brougham, and Series 75 as well as the Eldorado.

The Calais was really the direct descendant of the old Series 61 and inherited its role as the "economy" Cadillac, though the Calais wasn't priced that much less than the more popular DeVille. Calais production had started at a rate of around 20,000 units annually when the name appeared in 1965, but tapered off to around 7000 by 1974. Typically, only two models were listed, two- and four-door hardtops; the last Calais sedan (with fixed "B" post) was offered in 1967.

The DeVille was a four-model series from 1967 through 1971, when it too was reduced to just a hardtop coupe and sedan. A DeVille sedan with fixed "B" pillars was really a contradiction in terms, considering the history of the name, and possibly for that reason it was the least popular body style. The DeVille convertible was much more successful: Cadillac sold an encouraging 15,000 to 18,000 of these each year through 1970. But that was not enough to sustain one body style. When the Eldorado line added a convertible, it was felt the DeVille soft top was superfluous. Thus, the 1970 DeVille was the last standard six-

1967 Fleetwood 60 Special Brougham

1967 Coupe deVille

1968 Fleetwood Eldorado

1968 DeVille convertible

1968 Hardtop Sedan deVille

passenger Cadillac convertible.

Styling between 1967 and '74 can be divided into two main periods: the crisp, chiseled look of the 1967-70 models, and the more rounded appearance of the fully redesigned 1971-74 cars. Since the relatively low-volume Fleetwood models were too expensive to update drastically each year, this series retained the same body styles in each of these two generations. From 1967 through 1970, the 60 Special long-wheelbase sedan was augmented by the 60 Special Brougham; the rest of the line comprised the Eldorado and the Seventy-Five sedan and limousine. With Cadillac's 1971 redesign, the Brougham was retained, the 60 Special was dropped, and the Eldorado convertible was added. This lineup was continued through 1976.

The big mechanical news for 1968 was an all-new 472-cid V-8 which produced 375 bhp. The 472 was specifically designed to meet the then-new emission control standards and had been tested over half a million miles in the laboratory. Hidden wipers and federally required safety features like headrests and side marker lights were also made standard in '68.

In 1969, Cadillac set another calendar year pro-

continued on page 81

Showcase 1958 Eldorado Brougham photo (page 74) by Bud Juneau. All other photos courtesy Cadillac Motor Car Division.

1969 Fleetwood Eldorado

1969 Fleetwood 60 Special Brougham

1970 Coupe deVille

1970 Hardtop Sedan deVille

1968 Eldorado Biarritz Town Coupe showcar

1971 Fleetwood Eldorado convertible

1971 Sedan deVille

1972 Fleetwood Eldorado coupe

Cadillac

COLOR SHOWCASE II

Top: Wreath-and-Crest Mascot
Center: 1957 Series 62 Sedan deVille
Bottom: Eldorado Brougham Town Car prototype

Top: 1958 Eldorado Brougham
Center: 1959 Eldorado Brougham by Pininfarina
Bottom: Cyclone show car of 1959

Top: 1959 Eldorado Biarritz Convertible
Center: 1960 Series 60 Special Fleetwood
Bottom: 1961 Series 62 Convertible

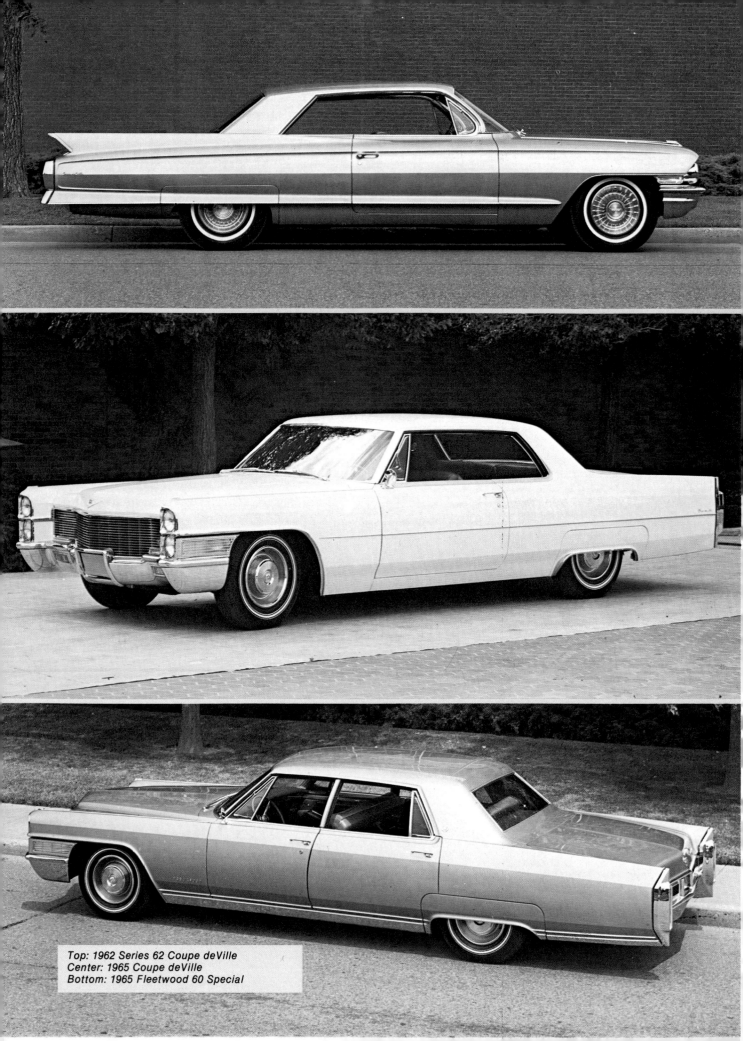

Top: 1962 Series 62 Coupe deVille
Center: 1965 Coupe deVille
Bottom: 1965 Fleetwood 60 Special

Top: 1967 Fleetwood Eldorado
Center: 1967 Fleetwood Eldorado
Bottom: 1971 Fleetwood Eldorado Convertible

Top: 1971 Fleetwood Brougham
Center: 1973 Coupe deVille
Bottom: 1975 Seville

Top: 1978 Fleetwood Eldorado
Center: 1977 Sedan deVille
Bottom: 1978 Coupe deVille

Top: 1980 Seville Elegante
Center: 1980 Eldorado Biarritz
Bottom: 1980 Coupe deVille

continued from page 72

duction record with 266,798 units, passing both Chrysler and AMC to achieve ninth place in industry totals. The '69 models had a squarer roofline, horizontal instead of vertical headlights, and wraparound front parking lights. Front vent windows were eliminated. Prices ranged from $5500 for the Calais to $11,000 for the Seventy-Five.

Cadillac developed a massive 500 cubic-inch V-8 for the 1970 Eldorado. This was the largest production passenger-car engine in the world and produced 400 horsepower (gross). Bias-ply fiberglass-belted tires became standard for all models as did a new type of radio antenna which was imbedded in the windshield glass.

The big redesign of 1971 included all-new styling for the Eldorado, which got a 6.3-inch longer wheelbase, a new perimeter frame, and coil-spring rear suspension. There was also a new bodyshell and revised styling for the DeVille, Calais, and Fleetwood. The '71s featured reinforced safety bumpers, a much stronger front-end structure, lower compression ratios, and flow-through ventilation.

From 1972 through '74, Cadillacs were little changed in appearance, as engineering and styling talent was heavily preoccupied with meeting the needs of the times: better crash protection, cleaner exhaust, and greater fuel economy. In some ways, the last two goals were quite difficult to reconcile in those years; the emphasis at Cadillac was on the emissions side. The design of both the 472- and 500-cid V-8s was amenable to emission control improvements. In 1973, for example, an exhaust gas recirculation system (EGR) was added to further reduce oxides of nitrogen (NOx) emissions, while revisions to engine pulleys and the air injection reactor (AIR) pump were incorporated to reduce engine noise.

The leader had remained the leader in these years although Cadillac sales, like those for the industry as a whole, slumped in 1973-74 in the wake of the Arab oil embargo. With the prospect of tightening gas supplies and higher per-gallon prices, American motorists were suddenly very concerned about fuel economy. Perhaps as a result of this, Cadillac's 1974 calendar year production fell to 230,649 cars, the lowest since 1970.

Better things were, however, in the making. An immediate sales recovery occurred throughout the industry in 1975, and Cadillac was readying a brand-new concept, a car which has since become yet another standard for the world. It was called Seville, but in no way did it resemble its finny, gas-guzzling namesake of the '50s.

1972 Sedan deVille

1973 Fleetwood Eldorado convertible

1973 Coupe deVille

1974 Fleetwood Eldorado coupe

1974 Fleetwood Brougham

1974 Coupe deVille

SPOTLIGHT: The Front-Wheel-Drive Eldorado

Among production Cadillacs the name Eldorado has always been reserved for the most distinctive models—the ones that pioneered the new ideas. When the name first appeared in 1953, it graced a rakish convertible with a dropped beltline and the industry's first panoramic wraparound windshield. In 1955, Eldorado ushered in the pointed tailfin styling which would remain popular in the late '50s and early '60s. In 1957 came the Eldorado Brougham. And 10 years after that, the fabulous front-drive Eldorado arrived—a car that is still with us today.

The original 1967 Eldorado is still the best-looking of this series. Trim, chiseled, beautifully balanced, it is strong testimony to the contention of then styling chief Bill Mitchell that large cars don't have to look big and clumsy. Mitchell and his designers took enormous pains to make the car as perfect as possible in every way. From end to end it displays no excess chrome, not a piece of silly ornamentation. It is a complete, integrated package. The busiest aspect of its design is the bold egg-crate grille which serves to hide the headlights (note the blanked-off sections at each end). But against the massively clean overall styling, the grille doesn't look at all out of place or out of proportion.

A lot of publicity attended the last Eldorado convertibles of 1976, which were pushed up way beyond their real value that year due to collector demand. Now that the dust has settled, it's likely the '76 convertible is not nearly as good an investment as an original '67 coupe—a prize Eldorado that would do justice to any collection.

Quarter-scale clay model for 1979 Eldorado

"The White Light of Publicity" 1975-1980

The pressure was on. In the second half of the '70s, a luxury-car maker could no longer afford to ignore the need to save energy—or buyer concern over gas mileage and rising fuel prices. While Cadillac continued to lead all other luxury makes in production by a wide margin in the last part of the decade, it was required to meet government fuel economy mandates or face unpalatable consequences. Those mandates (called the corporate average fuel economy or CAFE standards) may have been the best thing that ever happened to the industry. Certainly, this is true in Cadillac's case. The Arab oil embargo, and the fuel economy standards that followed, directly influenced development of the Seville.

Cadillac considered the name "Leland" for its new compact sedan, which would be released in 1975, but most managers felt the public wouldn't remember who Cadillac's founder was. Besides, Henry Leland had gone off and founded Lincoln. "LaSalle" was also in the running, but it too was rejected because of its "loser" image. Ultimately, the name Seville emerged as the preferred choice. In fact, it was such a good choice that Ford and Chrysler reacted with cars also bearing names of far-away places, Versailles and Cordoba. As for the car itself, Seville was squarely on target. According to chief engineer Robert Templin, "Cadillac is unique in GM in that it always knows where it wants to go. If there's growth in our end of the market, it's clear that we're to go after it."

Seville styling received mixed initial reviews. Overall, the car was clean and compact; its use of interior space compared favorably with Mercedes-Benz and BMW. But the rear roofline, a take-off on the style of the Rolls-Royce Silver Shadow, struck many observers as unimaginative and dull. "A more sloping backlight would probably intrude a little on trunk access," wrote one reviewer in 1977.

"Other than that, there's little that we can criticize. The slab sides, the taut, all-of-a-piece look to the front end, give the car [a] purposeful, road-hugging appearance . . ."

On the road, there was far less debate about this new $12,000 Cadillac. Seville's 350-cid V-8, mated to Cadillac's new electronic fuel injection system, delivered smooth, quick, turbine-like performance. From a dead stop, 60 mph came up in 10-11 seconds; top speed was better than 110 mph. The Seville's 1000-pound lower curb weight

1975 Seville

1975 Seville

and 27-inch shorter overall length compared to the '75 DeVille set the stage for GM's revolutionary downsized big cars which appeared two years later. But its compact size did not affect Seville's ride, which was typically Cadillac-smooth. The car was also extremely quiet, thanks to careful consideration and use of noise and vibration dampening techniques. Teflon leaf spring liners, rubber coil spring spacers, chambered shock absorbers, and body bolts locked with micro-encapsulated epoxy were responsible for effective sound deadening.

Even more impressive was how the Seville drove. It was almost certainly the best-handling Cadillac ever built, and much closer to its more expensive European competitors than their manu-

facturers liked to admit. There was some roll on corners, but nothing like the wallow typical of standard-sized Detroit cars. A Seville would not fly over washboard surfaces like a Mercedes 450 sedan, but it didn't cost as much, either. The Standard of the World was still the standard.

Evidently, the car buying public appreciated the Seville. In the car's first full model year of 1976, Cadillac sold over 43,000 copies, accounting for about 15 percent of total division production. By 1978, sales were up to 57,000 units, though the rest of the Cadillac line had kept pace so this still represented about 15 percent of total sales. But the Seville should not be judged by sales figures alone. More important was what it demonstrated to the industry: It proved that Cadillac was flexi-

1975 Calais sedan

1975 Coupe deVille

1975 Fleetwood Eldorado coupe (left) and convertible (right)

1976 Calais sedan

1976 Sedan deVille

84

ble, ready with new ideas for luxury cars that were right for the times.

Cadillac fielded a lineup of Calais, DeVille, and Fleetwood cars in 1975-76 which were unchanged in body type from 1974. Styling was updated, with rectangular headlamps and Seville-like grillework. In 1976, high customer demand resulted in the greatest sales year in Cadillac history with 304,485 units, the first time the division had exceeded the 300,000 mark. Said general manager Edward C. Kennard, "We're especially elated with the fourth quarter results because they signify the enthusiastic acceptance of the newly styled, fuel efficient 1977 models by our customers."

Indeed they did. Though the Calais series and the Eldorado convertible were absent in 1977-78,

the division did still better. Cadillac set its second consecutive calendar year production record in 1977 with 335,785 units, then promptly broke the record again with 350,813 cars the following year. Output for 1979 was less spectacular, owing to many factors outside Cadillac's control. But significantly, the division maintained its two to three percent market share, the same percentage of industry sales it had held for many years.

Perhaps only Cadillac among the high-priced makes could so drastically change its offerings yet keep setting new sales records. The 1977 models were completely redesigned inside and out: 8 to 12 inches shorter and an average of 950 pounds lighter than their 1976 counterparts. Said Kennard, "Our engineers accomplished dramatic

The "last convertible"–the '76 Fleetwood Eldorado

1976 Fleetwood Eldorado coupe

1976 Fleetwood Brougham

1976 Seville

1976 Coupe deVille

1977 Seville

1977 Fleetwood Eldorado coupe

Front-end proposal for '77 Fleetwood Brougham

1977 Coupe deVille

1978 Coupe deVille

1977 Sedan deVille

1978 Fleetwood Brougham

1978 Seville Elegante (production model)

1978 Eldorado Biarritz

1978 Eldorado Custom Biarritz Classic

1978 Seville Elegante showcar

weight savings in many areas of the new models through the use of advanced computerized technology and durable, lightweight materials." The '77s were powered by a cleaner, more efficient 425-cid V-8, except for the Seville which continued to use its 350-cid electronically fuel-injected engine.

The story for 1979 was much the same. The Eldorado, fully redesigned for the first time since 1971, was now thoroughly up to date. Its chassis was 224 pounds lighter and 20 inches shorter than in '78. Its wheelbase was 12 inches shorter and turning circle was about five feet tighter. The wheelbase was trimmed thanks to a new independent rear suspension, which made it possible to locate the rear wheels 10 inches further forward in the chassis with no loss of passenger space.

Cadillac's optional features for '79 included electrically controlled left and right outside rearview mirrors, a fully automatic radio antenna that lowered into the fender when the radio or ignition was turned off, eight-track or cassette stereo tape player, 40-channel CB radio, and the unique Tripmaster on-board computer system. First introduced as a DeVille option in 1978, Tripmaster provided digital readouts at the touch of a button

Toronado-like lines were tried on early clay for '79 Eldorado.

1979 Eldorado nears final form in March, 1976.

Note circular wheel cut-outs on this early scale model.

Rear view of above prototype reveals slanted trunklid.

Elegant simplicity—February, 1976 Eldorado mock-up

June, 1976 Eldorado grille proposal

This clay's "bustle-back" trunk would appear on 1980 Seville.

By September, 1976, production styling was nearly ready.

for average miles per gallon, average speed, miles to destination, estimated time of arrival, engine rpm, engine temperature, and electrical system voltage. It offers a glimpse at how electronics will be used in all cars of the future.

In 1980, Cadillac is still reaping "the white light of publicity," to no one's great surprise. Attention this year focuses on the striking new Seville, which now shares the Eldorado's front-wheel-drive chassis with four-wheel independent suspension. Yet the Seville's sophisticated under-pinnings are easily overshadowed by its spec-tacular new rear-end styling. The car's original notchback shape has been replaced with a vintage-style "trunkback" design inspired by the custom Hooper coachwork of 30 and 40 years ago. Without resorting to "throwback" design details like Virgil Exner's ugly free-standing headlights (as used on early '60s Imperials), designer Wayne Cady has come up with the most distinctive Cadillac since the '67 Eldorado. Again, America has produced a luxury car which looks like nothing else on the road.

There's already been a lot of controversy about the new Seville, as you might expect from its fairly radical design. But most observers who are aware of history think time is on its side. The latest Seville is an ideal luxury car for the fuel-short 1980s.

The reason Seville—like other 1980 Cadillacs—is so "right" for the new decade has to do with its motive power. Cadillac's new optional 368-cid V-8 with digital electronic fuel injection (DEFI) (not available on California cars) is a tremendous accomplishment. Its sensors monitor some two dozen operating variables like manifold pressure, barometric pressure, coolant temperature, manifold temperature, engine speed, and throttle position. The system processes this information and constantly adjusts engine running for optimum economy and performance regardless of

conditions. EPA fuel economy figures for the DEFI Seville are 19 mph highway and 14 mpg city, with a composite figure of 16.

Standard for Seville, and optional on other models, is the 350-cid diesel V-8, perhaps the most important luxury-car engine development since the valve-in-head Cadillac V-8 of 1949. This powerplant acts like no diesel ever did. Even when the engine is dead cold, there's a wait of only about 10 seconds while the glow plugs heat up. A polite chime tells you when the engine is ready to fire. Once warmed up, this engine gives hardly a hint that it's a diesel. There's no smell and little engine noise. Its mid-range performance is comparable to that of a gasoline-powered V-8 with

1979 Eldorado

1979 Eldorado

Cadillac engineers compare lines of modified '77 car (left) with proposed styling for 1979 (right).

1979 Fleetwood Brougham D'Elegance

1979 Special Edition "Phaeton"

somewhat less power. Most important of all, the diesel has an EPA rating of 29 highway, 21 city, with a composite of 24 mpg. In a big, luxurious car like the Sedan DeVille, this sort of economy is simply astounding. Cadillac has once again led the way for the industry. The division's 1980 models prove that it is possible to combine traditional size and luxury with the sort of fuel economy that used to be associated only with small, uncomfortable imports.

It would be nice, we think, to invite Henry Martyn Leland back to the company he founded 77 years ago. For his visit we'd order a Seville, of course: the first sedan to combine front-wheel drive, four-wheel independent suspension, four-wheel disc brakes, electronic level control, electronic climate control, standard diesel engine, and cruise control. We know Henry might frown at the thought of a diesel, but we think he would be impressed by what Cadillac has done with this engine—as much as we were, in fact. We would naturally make sure his Seville was of a conservative hue. We'd put him behind the wheel to go for a spin.

A modest celebration (no alcohol or tobacco, understand) would be held when Mr. Leland returned from his drive. We're inclined to think that would be in order: There's no doubt Henry Martyn Leland would strongly approve of the 1980 Cadillacs.

1979 Sedan deVille

1979 Seville Elegante

1980 Seville Elegante

1980 Seville Elegante

1980 Eldorado Biarritz

1980 Coupe deVille

1980 Fleetwood Brougham

1980 Fleetwood Brougham

SPOTLIGHT: 1980 Seville

You'll never mistake the 1980 Seville for anything else. In one swoop, Cadillac designer Wayne Cady transformed the previous innocuous notchback into the most dramatic-looking luxury car on the road. The classic rear-deck treatment with its razor-edge lines actually takes its inspiration from England's Hooper Coach Company, which used a similar styling theme for its coachbuilt cars in the late '40s and early '50s. The Vanden Plas Coachworks, now a part of British Leyland (BL), still produces a custom-built Daimler limousine with the same general configuration. But it's safe to say no Daimler ever looked this good.

The all-new second-generation Seville also features a sculptured hood and fender profile line leading into the "A" pillar, which tilts at a rakish new angle. A vertical grille leads the eye to a larger header and windsplit molding featuring an integral crest. A one-piece bumper with integral bumper guards cradles the grille. Horizontal taillights, flared wheel openings, new cast aluminum wheels with brushed chrome hubcaps, optional wire wheels, and an "Elegante" option with striking two-tone paint complete the package.

Well, the visual package anyway. Mechanically, the 1980 Seville is the first and only American production

car to combine front-wheel drive, independent four-wheel suspension, four-wheel disc brakes, electronic leveling control, climate control, a standard diesel V-8 engine, and cruise control. And you were thinking of spending $15,000 more to buy a Mercedes?

90

"That Which Deserves to Live—Lives"
Cadillacs for Collectors

Cadillac was a slow starter as a collector car, though things are quite different now. The Antique- and Classic-era models were mainly spoken for years ago, so they're going to be prohibitively expensive for the average collector today. The postwar models are where the action is, though some are more collectible than others. Surprisingly, a few highly touted Cadillacs aren't really collectible at all.

The early postwar Fleetwood 75 long-wheelbase cars have recently been granted Classic status by the Classic Car Club of America. That was a good decision for they are impressive machines. Series 75s came in a variety of body styles, all on a 147-inch wheelbase. Available offerings included the five-passenger sedan, seven-passenger sedan and Imperial, and a nine-passenger Business sedan and Business Imperial. These were big, luxurious cars, beautifully finished, and are among the few affordable true Classics left.

In 1950, the 75s were given a new body and updated styling like that used on the rest of the line since '48. In 1949, the 75 still had its prewar body but received the new short-stroke ohv V-8 introduced that year for all Cadillacs. Because this engine differed markedly from the older L-head engine, prices of 1949 75s have lagged behind those of earlier models. The ohv V-8 is considered the better power unit by most engineers, but among collectors its running quality versus that of the smooth old L-head is debated. As a result, the '49 is a better buy for someone on a budget who prefers the "old school" design.

Turning to early postwar standard-wheelbase Cadillacs, the convertibles and fastback coupes stand out. The fastback or sedanet was attractive both before and after the 1948 restyle. Coupes trail convertibles in price by a good 50 percent at current market values, and would be better buys for collectors interested in the 1946-47 generation. (The 1942 models, which shared the same body with the 1946-47s, are much more rare owing to limited production and are therefore quite valuable.)

It is impossible to overrate the 1948 Cadillac, which was an industry landmark in styling. As the progenitor of not only the tailfin but also a long line of future Cadillacs, the '48 ranks as the most collectible post-1945 model. It also possesses a trait typical of many first-year designs: It was by far the cleanest version of this bodyshell, which was used through 1953. After 1949, styling gradually became gaudier and paunchier in response to what Cadillac saw as the will of the public. Happily, the 1948s were only mildly facelifted for '49. So, compared to the 1950-53 editions, the 1948-49s have a commanding lead in market value, a lead which will probably lengthen as the years pass.

As in previous eras certain body styles are considered more desirable than others. Here, the 1948-49 sedanets and convertibles are the most sought-after models. Equally important is the 1949 Coupe deVille, the first pillarless Cadillac. Convertibles are rapidly appreciating in value, but a sedanet or Coupe deVille can be found for slightly less than a soft top.

Despite its more modern engine, the 1949 Cadillac does not seem to have as much appeal for collectors as the '48. If anything, the latter is preferred. Interestingly, both '48 and '49 Series 61 and 62 coupes, convertibles, and Coupe deVille along with the 60 Special are rated as Milestones by the Milestone Car Society. Yet despite this, the 1948-49s do not always command higher prices than their 1946-47 counterparts.

The year 1953 saw another stand-out—the limited-production Eldorado convertible. This car had a hotted-up 210-bhp engine and was offered in a choice of four exterior colors (red, blue, white, and ochre) with a color-keyed leather interior. It shared GM's supercar spotlight that year with Buick's Skylark and Oldsmobile's Fiesta. Of the three, the Skylark was the most plentiful with a production run of 1690, while only 532 Eldorados and 490 Fiestas were built. This first Eldorado probably commands the highest collector interest and market value of any Cadillac from the 1946-56 period. Its low production means continued price increases in the future, so it is definitely a model to look for.

Cadillac Values: A General Guide

There are numerous vintage-auto price guides on the market, some purporting to give prices to the nearest $50 in a half-dozen different condition classes for every model and body style ever made. Because of its small scale compared to the used-car field and the wide variety in condition of the cars available, the vintage-car market is practically impossible to categorize that way. The best a price guide can do is put you in the ballpark: It can outline a *general* area where the price *should* be (always subject to exceptions, like an "extremely rare" or "desirable" body style) based on the opinions of experts, collectors, and known sales. This is what we have attempted to do here.

For more information you may wish to order the *Old Cars Price Guide,* Krause Publications, Iola, Wisconsin 54945; the *Old Car Value Guide,* 910 Tony Lama Street, El Paso, Texas 47401; the *C.P.I. Guide (Cars of Particular Interest),* Box 11409, Baltimore, Maryland 21230; and/or the *Collector Car Auction Reporter,* Box 1399, Bloomington, Indiana 47401. If you are interested in precise pricing information, it is essential to compare the values listed in several of these publications. "Asking prices," particularly in the old-car classified columns, cannot be relied upon.

CONSUMER GUIDE® magazine's Cadillac value estimates are divided into three categories. "Fair" means a restorable car, perhaps with some nonstructural rust or body damage, possibly not complete mechanically or bodily, probably not roadworthy, and possibly not even running. "Good" refers to a running car, either original or an old restoration, complete in every way including mechanical components, body parts, and accessories, but possibly with some minor rust or body damage. "Excellent" means an original unrestored or authentically restored car capable of achieving 85 percent or higher in concours judging, with no rust or body damage, of course, and not defective in any way.

Each category presents price ranges, and sometimes these are rather wide. The reason for this is model and body style variations. Among models from the Classic era (1925-42), Fleetwood custom bodies usually bring more than Fisher bodies. Open cars typically lead closed styles in price by a long way: A Fisher roadster is worth far more than a Fleetwood sedan of the same model, for example. Among prewar open models, roadsters enjoy a price lead even over convertible sedans and touring cars.

No matter what they say on television, every old car is *not* worth half-a-million dollars. Aside from informing you of that, we hope this value guide will provide you with an idea of what to look for if you're looking, or what to ask for if you're selling.

Year and Model	Fair	Good	Excellent
1903-08 Single-cylinder	$2,500-3,500	$5,500-6,500	$11,000-13,000
1904-08 Four-cylinder	3,000-4,000	6,000-7,000	14,000-16,000
1909-14 Thirty	3,500-4,500	6,500-7,500	10,000-18,000
1915-25 V-8	2,500-3,500	6,500-7,500	10,000-15,000
1926-32 V-8 (inc. LaSalle)	5,000-7,000	8,000-17,000	20,000-30,000
1930-37 V-12	3,000-8,000	7,500-10,000	10,000-35,000
1930-38 V-16	5,000-10,000	15,000-25,000	18,000-50,000
1939-41 V-16	4,000-6,000	8,000-12,000	15,000-30,000
1934-41 V-8 (inc. LaSalle)	1,500-4,000	5,000-9,500	10,000-20,000
1938-40 60 Special	1,800-2,000	4,000-6,000	8,500-10,000
1941 60 Special	2,000-3,000	4,000-10,000	10,000-15,000
1942-47	500-1,500	2,000-3,000	4,000-8,000
1948-49	750-1,200	1,800-2,500	4,000-7,000
1950-57	500-1,000	1,200-2,000	3,500-7,000
1953 Eldorado	1,500-2,000	3,500-4,500	9,000-11,000
1954-56 Eldorado	1,000-1,500	2,500-3,500	5,000-7,500
1957-58 Eldorado Brougham	1,800-2,200	4,000-5,000	9,000-12,000
1958-66	300-800	1,000-2,000	2,500-5,000
1959-60 Eldorado Brougham	500-1,000	1,500-2,500	3,500-4,500
1957-66 Eldorado	1,000-1,200	2,000-2,500	4,000-5,000
1967-69 Eldorado	500-1,000	1,500-2,000	3,000-4,000
1970-76 Eldorado coupe	1,000-1,500	2,500-3,500	5,000-6,000
1970-76 Eldorado convertible	2,000-2,500	3,000-4,000	7,500-10,000
1975-76 Seville	1,000-2,000	2,000-3,000	7,000-8,000

Eldorado convertibles were also offered for 1954 and '55 with increasingly powerful engines. The 1955 edition had 270 bhp and there were two 305-bhp models for 1956, the Seville hardtop and the Biarritz convertible. Significantly, the 1954-56 Eldorados sold for about $1500 less than the '53 version. Because of their greater numbers and less unique styling, they haven't captured the enthusiasm of collectors the way the '53 has. In choosing one of these models, consider styling as it will influence asking price and future appreciation potential. A major restyle occurred in 1954 with heavier, bulkier-looking lines and more garish trim inside and out. Eldorados gained shark-like tailfins in 1955, and these have their enthusiasts and detractors.

In 1957, Cadillac unleashed a surprise with its ultra-complex and now highly coveted Eldorado Brougham, priced new at $13,074 and billed as the last word in automobiles. Only 704 copies were built in 1957-58, and the Brougham has since become the most desired of all postwar Cadillacs. Prices paid recently have been phenomenal—almost equal to those paid for open cars from the Classic era.

Chief among the Brougham's technical novelties was its air suspension system which used a rubber dome or air chamber at each wheel instead of conventional springs. The air chambers were pumped up by a small motor and regulated by three levelers to maintain constant ride height regardless of road or load conditions. Brougham enthusiasts swear there's nothing like the "air-spring ride," especially on rough roads. But insufficient research and development virtually guaranteed unreliability: The domes would blow out or spring leaks at the drop of a hat, causing many a Brougham to drop down on its haunches. As a result, many frustrated owners eventually resorted to conventional coil springs (dealer installed at a cost of about $400) and most Broughams survive today without their original air domes.

A history of service trouble does not deter collectors, however. Their concern with authenticity means that original air-suspension Broughams will carry a price premium over cars that have been converted. Indeed, some enthusiasts have actually attempted to convert modified cars *back* to original specification. However, the Brougham's very limited production run has made this distinction less important lately. All Eldorado Brougham owners are guaranteed admiration from their fellow enthusiasts. And whenever an owner decides to sell, there will usually be a long line of people ready and willing to pay.

For 1959 and 1960, the Eldorado Brougham was built in Italy by Pininfarina with coachwork which was hard to tell at a glance from the standard Cadillacs. Only 200 were built in this period, but their greater rarity hasn't compensated for higher

Available & Affordable	Compared to:
1946-47	
61/62 coupe	62 convertible
62 convertible	prewar convertibles
75 sedans/limousine	prewar 75 models
1948	
61/62 coupe	1946-47 62 convertible
60 Special	1946-47 60 Special
75 sedan/limousine	prewar 75 models
1949	
61/62 coupe	62 convertible
62 Coupe de Ville	62 convertible
60 Special	1948 60 Special
75 long sedan/limousine	pre-1949 75 models
1953-56	
1954-56 Eldorado convertible	1953 Eldorado
Eldorado hardtops	Eldorado convertibles
1967-80	
1967-70 Eldorado hardtop	1971-77 Eldorados
1971-75 Eldorado convertibles	1976 Eldorado convertible

collector interest in the earlier versions. This is one of the few instances where a lower-production model is less sought-after. Of course, by Cadillac standards Brougham production in all years was infinitesimal.

Interest in late '50s and early '60s Cadillacs is growing slowly, though it is hard to single out any real sleepers yet. This is partly because many are still in everyday service and haven't shown up on the collector market. The Eldorado Biarritz convertible and Seville hardtop were continued through 1960, after which only the convertible was offered. In 1965, the Eldorado became a Fleetwood series, and in 1967, it appeared with a new body and front-wheel drive, both derived from the Olds Toronado.

The 1967 Eldorado was as significant in its day as the 1948 "tailfin" model or the 1949 V-8. Necessarily, it is destined to be highly prized by collectors and is more valuable than standard Cadillacs of the same period. The years to watch for are the early ones, the 1967-70 models. After this, the car became larger, longer, wider, fatter, and less agile. A soft-top version was offered from 1971, but by then the convertible market was drying up fast. This was due to the continued popularity of air conditioning and hardtops over the years, plus rumors that the government would enact safety standards which would effectively ban the sale of cars without rollover protection: namely, convertibles. In 1976, Cadillac found itself the only domestic car maker with a soft-top model in its catalog.

The last Eldorado convertible rolled off the line on April 21, 1976. This car was identical to 199 preceeding examples, all specially painted to mark the occasion; it was retained by Cadillac for historical purposes. General manager Edward C. Kennard noted that 1976 production was actually higher than in 1975 (14,000 versus 8950). The end, he said, was forced by the demise of Cadillac's top supplier: "Cadillac bought every available convertible top two years ago, and this proved enough to manufacture exactly 14,000 1976 convertibles."

The company made a lot of noise about its final convertible, but later came to regret it. Even before the last ones were built, dealers were deluged with more orders than they could possibly fill. Soon, speculators were hawking convertibles for two or three times their sticker price. Cries of "collectors item" were rampant.

It's a free country, and everyone has the right to act foolish. But CONSUMER GUIDE® magazine would be unworthy of its name if we didn't attempt to apply a little modest "horse sense." First, the '76 Eldorado wasn't the last American convertible strictly speaking, because AMC still builds a removable-hardtop Jeep. Second, the importance of this car as an artifact of automotive history has been diluted by a host of small, specialist coachbuilders who began snipping off the tops of Eldorado and standard Cadillac coupes right after the factory quit making its own convertibles. Third, there were altogether too many '76 Eldorado convertibles built for them to be considered true collector's items yet.

Consider that against those 14,000 '76 convertibles there were only 704 1957-58 Eldorado Broughams built. When new, both models were priced at about the same level (though inflation made the price of the '76 somewhat higher in gross dollars). Yet the Brougham took 20 years to exceed its original list price on the collector market. Our guess is that it may be the year 2000 before the '76 Eldorado convertible becomes scarce enough to be noticed by serious collectors. Because many owners have already put their cars in mothballs as a future investment, mint '76s may actually be a lot more commonplace in a few years than the lower-production, "less worthy" 1975 Eldorado convertibles.

Our advice is to stick with the '40s, '50s, and '60s if you're interested in Cadillacs as collector's items or investments. Your emphasis, and your search, should be for the 1948-49 fastback, hardtop, and convertible; the 1953 Eldorado; the 1957-58 Eldorado Brougham; and the 1967-70 Eldorado. As for the 1976 Eldorado convertible, take a tip from the Smithsonian Institution in Washington. Cadillac offered to donate its very last convertible to the museum: The Smithsonian politely declined.

Cadillac Production Figures

MODEL YEAR 1903-1942

Single-cylinder models		Total
1903-08	A, B, E, F, K, M, S, T	13,981

Four-cylinder models		
1905-08	D, G, H, L	1,344
1909	Thirty	5,903
1910	Thirty	8,008
1911	Thirty	10,018
1912	Thirty	13,995
1913	Thirty	15,018
1914	Thirty	14,002

Eight-cylinder models		
1915	51	13,002
1916	53	18,004
1917	55	18,002
1918	57	20,285
1919	57	20,678
1920	59	19,628
1921	59	5,250
1922	61	26,296
1923	61	14,707
1924	V-63	18,827
1925	V-63	16,673

Eight-cylinder models, continued		Total
1926	314	14,249
1927	314A	36,369
1928	341, 341A	40,000
1929	341B	18,004
1930	353	11,005
1931	355	10,709
1932	355B	2,693
1933	355C	2,096
1934	355D	5,080
1935	10	3,209
1936	60, 70, 75	11,927
1937	60, 65, 70, 75	13,629
1938	60, 60S, 65, 75	8,957
1939	61, 60S, 75	13,445
1940	62, 60S, 72, 75	12,985
1941	61, 62, 63, 60S, 67, 75	66,130
1942	61, 62, 63, 60S, 67, 75	16,511

Twelve-cylinder models		
1930-31	370, 370A	5,725
1932	370B	1,709
1933	370C	952

Twelve-cylinder models, continued

Year	Model	Total
1934	370D	683
1935	370D (40)	377
1936	80, 85	901
1937	85	474

Sixteen-cylinder models

Year	Model	Total
1930-31	452, 452A	3,250
1932	452B	296
1933	452C	125
1934	452D	56
1935	452D (60)	50
1936	90	52
1937	90	49
1938	90	311
1939	90	136
1940	90	61

LaSalle

Eight-cylinder models

Year	Model	Total
1927	303	10,767
1928	303	16,038
1929	328	22,961
1930	340	14,986
1931	345A	10,095
1932	345B	3,386
1933	345C	3,482
1934	350	7,195
1935	50	8,651
1936	50	13,004
1937	50	32,000
1938	50	15,575
1939	50	22,001
1940	50, 52	24,130

MODEL YEAR 1946-1979

Year	Series 61	Series 62	Series 60 Special	Series 75	75 comm. chassis	Eldorado	Eldorado Brougham	Calais	DeVille	fwd. Eldorado cpe.	fwd. Eldorado conv.	Seville
1946	3,001	18,566	5,700	365	1,292							
1947	8,555	39,835	8,500	2,410	2,626							
1948	8,603	34,213	6,561	1,260	2,069							
1949	22,148	55,643	11,400	1,501	1,862							
1950	26,772	59,818	13,755	1,460	2,052							
1951	4,700	54,596	18,631	2,205	2,960							
1952		70,255	16,110	2,200	1,694							
1953		84,914	20,000	2,200	2,005	532						
1954		75,195	16,200	1,500	1,635	2,150						
1955		114,636	18,300	1,916	1,975	3,950						
1956		127,452	17,000	2,050	2,025	6,050						
1957		114,472	24,000	1,900	2,169	3,900	400					
1958		103,457	12,900	1,532	1,915	1,670	304					
1959		124,126	12,250	1,400	2,102	2,295	99					
1960		124,213	11,800	1,550	2,160	2,360	101					
1961		117,600	15,500	1,625	2,204	1,450						
1962		142,160	13,350	1,600	2,280	1,450						
1963		143,347	14,000	1,475	2,527	1,825						
1964		145,475	14,550	1,425	2,639	1,870						
1965			18,100	1,250	2,669	2,125		34,211	123,080			
1966			18,805	2,017	2,463	2,250		28,680	142,190			
1967			16,300	1,800	2,333			21,830	139,807	17,930		
1968			18,600	1,800	2,413			18,190	164,472	24,528		
1969			19,845	2,036	2,550			12,425	163,048	23,333		
1970			18,651	2,116	2,506			9,911	181,719	23,842		
1971			15,200	1,600	2,014			6,929	135,426	20,568	6,800	
1972			20,750	1,915	2,462			7,775	194,811	32,099	7,975	
1973			24,800	2,060	2,212			8,073	216,243	42,136	9,315	
1974			18,250	1,900	2,265			6,883	172,620	32,812	7,600	
1975			18,755	1,851	1,328			8,300	173,570	35,802	8,950	16,355
1976			24,500	1,815	1,509			6,200	182,159	35,184	14,000	43,772
1977			28,000	2,614	1,299				234,171	47,344		45,060
1978			36,800	1,530	852				206,701	46,816		56,985
1979			42,200	2,025	864				215,101	67,436		53,487

**Bibliography & Sources
for Further Reading**

Cadillac 1902-1961 (History in Ads), by Griffiths & Phillips, P/G Publications, 317 Quaker Ridge Road, Timonium MD 21903

Cadillacs of the Forties, by Roy A. Schneider, Heritage House, Post Office Box 7, Temple City CA 91780

Cadillac: The Complete History, by Maurice D. Hendry, Automobile Quarterly Publications, 215 W. Main St., Kutztown PA 19530

Sixteen Cylinder Motorcars, by Roy A. Schneider, Heritage House, Post Office Box 7, Temple City CA 91780

Car Collector/Car Classics magazine, Box 28571, Atlanta GA 30326

Special-Interest Autos magazine, Box 196, Bennington VT 05201

The Milestone Car magazine, Box 50850, Indianapolis IN 46250

The Self-Starter magazine, 3340 Poplar Drive, Warren MI 48091

Clubs for Cadillac Enthusiasts

Brougham Owners Association (1957-60 Eldorado Brougham owners only), 1690 Monroe Drive N.E., Atlanta GA 30324

Cadillac Convertible Owners of America (convertible owners or prospective owners), Post Office Box 920, Thiells, NY 10984

Cadillac-LaSalle Club Inc. (all models 25 years old or older), 3340 Poplar Drive, Warren MI 48091

Acknowledgments

Special thanks to Lon Huffman of Cadillac Division Public Relations, Detroit, for kind assistance in source materials and photographs. Portions of Chapter II by Roy A. Schneider appeared in *Car Classics,* February 1977. Chapter III by Jeffrey I. Godshall appeared in *Special-Interest Autos,* May-June 1971. Portions of Chapter VI by Richard M. Langworth appeared in *Cars & Parts* magazine, November 1978. Portions of Chapter X by Richard M. Langworth appeared in *Car Classics,* February 1977.

Eldorado Brougham Town Car shared '56 Motorama spotlight with Oldsmobile Golden Rocket (above left) and Pontiac Club deMer (above right).